LIFE SCIENCE LIBRARY

THE MIND

LIFE SCIENCE LIBRARY

CONSULTING EDITORS
René Dubos
Henry Margenau
C. P. Snow

THE MIND

by John Rowan Wilson
and the Editors of LIFE

TIME INCORPORATED, NEW YORK

ABOUT THIS BOOK

MANY SCIENCES are contributing to an understanding of that elusive subject summed up as "the mind," and many of the findings of most of them are set in this volume. The emphasis, however, falls chiefly on two fields of scientific inquiry: neurology and psychology. In text chapters and picture essays, the book describes the anatomy of the nervous system and summarizes the most recent research into such subjects as learning, intelligence and mental illness. It explores the future of the mind—and perhaps of man—as glimpses of it are caught in experimental laboratories today.

Chapters of text alternate with picture essays which illustrate or complement the chapters, although each may be read independently. For example, Chapter 4, "Psychoanalysis: Delving into the Unconscious," is followed by a photographic album of the life of Sigmund Freud, the founder of the psychoanalytic method.

THE AUTHOR

JOHN ROWAN WILSON is an English surgeon, novelist and medical journalist who has been serving as assistant editor of the *British Medical Journal*, the official publication of the British Medical Association, since 1962. He studied medicine at the University of Leeds after reading Somerset Maugham's advice that medicine was the best career for anyone who wanted to write. A ship's doctor in the British Merchant Navy from 1946 to 1948, he has also served as a medical director for the Lederle Division of American Cyanamid Company. Dr. Wilson is the author of six books, including *Margin of Safety*, which deals with poliomyelitis.

THE CONSULTING EDITORS

RENE DUBOS, member and professor of The Rockefeller University, is a microbiologist and experimental pathologist world-famous for his pioneering in antibiotics, including the discovery of tyrothricin. He has written *Man Adapting*, and is a co-author of *Health and Disease* in this series.

HENRY MARGENAU is Eugene Higgins professor of physics and natural philosophy at Yale, editor of the *American Journal of Science* and a contributor to spectroscopy and nuclear physics. He has written *The Nature of Physical Reality*, and he is coauthor of *The Scientist* in this series.

C. P. SNOW, physicist and author, has won an international audience for his novels, including *The New Men*, *The Search*, *The Affair* and *Corridors of Power*, which explore the scientist's role in contemporary society. As Lord Snow, he was named a member of the British Ministry of Technology in 1964.

ON THE COVER

The picture of an eager eight-year-old absorbed in the process of learning was taken during a third-grade class at Hunter Elementary School in New York City. On the back cover is a drawing of an animal maze, one of the most useful tools of experimental psychology.

CONTENTS

The text for the chapters of this book was written by John Rowan Wilson, for the picture essays by the editorial staff. The following individuals and departments of Time Inc. were helpful in the production of the book: Larry Burrows, Ralph Crane, Alfred Eisenstaedt, Eliot Elisofon, Fritz Goro, Yale Joel, Robert W. Kelley, Dmitri Kessel, Ralph Morse, LIFE staff photographers; Dorothy B. Seiberling, LIFE Associate Editor; George Karas, Chief, LIFE Photographic Laboratory; Margaret Sargent, LIFE film editor; Doris O'Neil, Chief, LIFE Picture Library; Richard M. Clurman, Chief of the TIME-LIFE News Service; and Peter Draz, Chief of the Bureau of Editorial Reference.

INTRODUCTION

To LEARN ABOUT THE MIND we must begin with introspection, or observation of our own experience. We can also collect indirect evidence by studying the behavior of our fellow men and fellow creatures.

Imagine we are strolling together in my garden. From your reactions and your comments, I can divine much of your feeling and thinking, and much concerning your general mood. A rose may attract your attention. By perceiving the color, the smell, the stab of the thorn, you form an impression of this yellow rose in your mind, and this impression promptly merges with past impressions. The rose in your mind is bound to be similar to the rose in mine, but they are not identical, because no two minds are ever the same.

Our impressions are incorporated into our memories, and thus form the body of our experience. Our individual behavior is determined by the combination of new impressions with the memory of previous experiences. The mind can handle complex situations through the use of abstraction and combination, and reach logical conclusions which may result in decisive action or creative ideas.

The way intentions can be accurately executed in skilled movements —think of a surgeon, a pianist, a marksman—provides commonplace evidence of the correlation of the mental and the physical.

From clinical experience as well as experiments on animals, we know that certain behavior patterns are associated with well-defined areas in the brain. Through electrical stimulation of the brainstem and contiguous areas we can elicit the reactions of defense, flight and hunger; through stimulation of higher levels, a compulsion to laugh; through stimulation of the cortex, visual and auditory reactions, among others.

The results of this kind of research on the brain, which is among the subjects set forth in this volume, are fascinating but we must realize that they are hardly even a beginning. The great gap to be bridged in our knowledge of the mind remains this: how are the actions of the nervous system translated into consciousness?

—W. R. Hess
University of Zurich
Nobel Prizewinner in Medicine, 1949

1

The Elusive
Mind
of Man

INDESCRIBABLY BUSY
The man shown above is sitting in wide-eyed concentration over work brought home from the office—to give it his full attention. Though he is sitting almost motionless in a chair, he is nevertheless intensely busy. His mind is performing a number of tasks with familiar names —thinking, recalling, perceiving, deciding—but which are difficult to describe with precision.

Man's mind and his mental processes have always seemed to him as mysterious and fascinating as the universe itself, but investigation of the nature of the mind has become the province of experimental science only during relatively recent times. The scientific approach has paid increasingly rich dividends in knowledge, however. During the last century much new light has been cast on the nature of mental processes, on the sources of emotional life and on various patterns of behavior. And as new knowledge has been added, old, simple views have been replaced by more and more complicated questions. Nevertheless, man still asks, what *is* "mind"? Will all the mysteries disappear when we understand the functioning of the complex anatomical structure we know as the nervous system? Or does the mind have mysteries of its own?

The early Greek view of the mind was simplicity itself: the mind was the organ that was concerned only with pure ideas. Plato explicitly denied that it had anything to do with sensation. In his view, sensation was the function of the lowly body, which had no intellectual functions whatever. Aristotle had considerably more respect for the body. He believed that it was governed by psychic powers that were well worth the philosopher's attention, powers associated with motion and sensation. His anatomical knowledge was so primitive that he believed the physical seat of mental life was the heart rather than the brain, yet he anticipated modern thought in his belief that the living flesh was mysteriously animated by psychic powers.

The early Christians admired Plato more than they did Aristotle, and throughout the Middle Ages it was considered that the soul was the concern of God and the body the concern of the devil. Only the soul could know God's truth. After Aristotle, 2,000 years went by before another great philosopher reopened the old question with a new spirit of inquiry. He was René Descartes, born in France in 1596.

In Descartes' lifetime a series of discoveries about the nature of the world rocked and stimulated the mind of Renaissance man. The Polish astronomer Copernicus had died some 50 years before Descartes was born, but his theory that the earth was a planet revolving about the sun was still in hot dispute. In Descartes' time, William Gilbert published a monumental study of magnetism, and declared that the earth itself was a great magnet. Men of genius were finding the physical world fascinating, and they ventured beyond medieval dogmas for explanations of its origin. They began to look at the world to see what they could learn about it. Johannes Kepler formulated planetary laws, Galileo Galilei stated the basic laws of mechanics and William Harvey did his momentous investigation of the blood system. Francis Bacon articulated rules for proper scientific investigation, which he postulated as an experimental approach that accepted nothing on faith. Isaac Newton, who would build on Kepler and Galileo to discover many of the basic laws of physics, was born during this period and the telescope and compound microscope appeared upon the scene.

Descartes' active mind took the whole province of knowledge as his study. He worked in mathematics, physiology and mechanics as well as philosophy. He was a devout Christian, and his philosophy was a bold attempt to reconcile scientific methods with faith in God, to accommodate both a mechanistic view of the material world and an acknowledgment that the world was God's creation. He sought to use scientific methods to prove truths about the mind as well as about matter. Hence his famous dictum, "I think, therefore I am"; i.e., the existence of the mind was not revealed doctrine, but clearly observable fact. Descartes defined thinking as the whole range of conscious mental processes: intellectual thoughts, feelings, sensations and will. He believed the mind was always at work, even during sleep.

Descartes made a complete and total division between mind and body —one far more drastic than Plato's, who had at least assigned sensation to the body. Yet he performed an invaluable service by assigning *all* of man's animating processes to the mind. Once the inclusive nature of the mind was admitted, a host of new problems arose, many of which remain unanswered today. If the mind was accepted as the knower of all the enormously complex affairs of life, how did it know them? Knowledge was still conceived of as an accumulation of static "ideas," even though sensations were now included as part of knowledge. It was as though the head were seen as a storeroom which was suddenly found to be stuffed with all kinds of furniture. All of it—everything we know about the external world—had to be accounted for.

A small supply of furniture

Descartes' attempts to maintain a rigorously scientific attitude led him to be most cautious in accounting for the mind's contents. He said that the mind seemed to receive some ideas from outside itself, to invent others and to have some that were innate. The notion of innate ideas—of a mind born with a small basic supply of furniture—was one of the first of Descartes' ideas to come under attack. The attacker was the British philosopher John Locke, the most important spokesman for the school of hardheaded realists known as the empiricists. He conceded the mind no divinely bestowed furnishings at all.

The next few generations of philosophers were deeply caught up in the problems of how we know things, and thus in the problems of sensation. At the same time, the sciences, flourishing on every hand, were also closing in on sensation. Physiologists were not only discovering a great deal about how the sense organs work, they also attempted to study "psychic" phenomena such as stimulus and response. Inevitably, the two psychologically oriented fields, philosophy and physiology, coalesced.

The birth of experimental psychology is sometimes dated from the morning of October 22, 1850. On that day a German professor, Gustav Theodor Fechner, stayed late in bed, worrying about the materialistic tendencies of his times. Fechner had outstanding qualifications for bringing science and philosophy together. Educated first as a physician, he turned to physics, became seriously ill, underwent a religious conversion, and shifted his interest to mental and spiritual life. Just two years before, he had published a book on the mental life of flowers. He was a mystic trained in scientific method, more than a little odd, and on the morning in question it seemed to him a great pity that the mind and its relation to matter should be beyond the reach of scientific measurement. Then it occurred to him that it might not be beyond reach after all. Ten years later he published his *Elements of Psychophysics*, a text on the "exact science of the functional relations . . . between body and mind."

A noticeable difference

Fechner's contribution to psychology consists mainly of his inventive technique for measuring mental processes. For example, he asked a subject to look at a light of a certain intensity. Gradually the light was decreased until the subject reported a "just noticeable difference" in brightness. Fechner measured the physical intensity of the light at this stage, and the difference between the two intensities became a statistical unit of sensation. This unit is now known as a "jnd," the acronym taken from the English wording of "just noticeable difference." With a jnd as his yardstick, Fechner thought he could measure the intensity of sensation.

Fechner was followed by another German scholastic, 31 years his junior, who devoted the whole of a long life and voluminous works to the development of psychology as a distinct experimental science.

Like Fechner, Wilhelm Wundt was a physician turned philosopher. A confirmed experimentalist, he arrived at the University of Leipzig in 1875 to teach philosophy. There, four years later, he founded the first formal psychological laboratory in the world. By the time of his death in 1920, the science of psychology had been created, given shape and direction. Students came from all over the world, including America, to attend his courses. The impression he left was memorable—and in the course of leaving it he undoubtedly did much to foster the old international caricature of the German professor as pedantic, humorless and utterly intent on his work.

Wundt's prime interest was in sensation. He concentrated on this because he believed that the only mental functions that could be explored in the laboratory had to be as simple as sensations. His goal was to

A UNIVERSE WITHIN THE MIND

Robert Fludd, 17th Century English physician and inventor, theorized that the mind of man was a universe in miniature, as shown in this contemporary illustration. Fludd's universe was composed of a trinity of God, earth and man. Man's mind was composed of a corresponding trinity—intellect, imagination and sensation, the three large circles pictured outside the head. They combined inside the head to form various parts of the mind.

break down experience into elements of sensation. Students in his laboratory listened to metronomes, stared at flashing lights, poked one another with needles and reported in enthusiastic detail what they heard, saw and felt.

Beginning at the age of 21, Wundt wrote a total of 53,735 pages—the equivalent of more than a 500-page book every year for 100 years—and there is a tendency for later psychologists who have been obliged to read his works to speak of them with despair. As George A. Miller of Harvard says, "The sheer bulk of his writing made Wundt almost immune to criticism. A critic would be outwritten, evaded by qualifications, and buried under mountains of detail."

Wundt was a descendant of Descartes and John Locke insofar as he was trying to provide a means for describing the "ideas" of sensation, or the basic pieces of furniture in a man's head. He was like a man trying to describe a chair by measuring in meticulous detail its visual appearance, describing the sensations of touch it provided, and even what it sounded like when dragged across the room—but never considering what the purpose of the chair was. He was exhaustive, but somehow interesting points forever eluded him.

The great William James

Wundt's limitations were recognized well within his lifetime. Another German, Franz Brentano, published several books during the same period in which he took the position that sensation could be described only as an act, not as an "idea." Other voices soon began to speak up. Psychology was born in Germany, but it quickly became an international science, flourishing with particular vigor in America. A giant figure among American psychologists, a man who still inspires all schools, was William James, that literate and intuitive analyst of consciousness.

James was the oldest son of a large, well-to-do New York family. His father, Henry James Sr., believed in and practiced spirited and opinionated dinner-table conversation. He made many trips abroad with his family to broaden his children's education. William James's brother Henry Jr. was to become famous as a novelist. "Willy" at one point wished to become an artist. When he finally settled down to study science at Harvard, a teacher remarked that he was inclined to "unsystematic excursions" in unpredictable directions. Eventually he attained a medical degree. He was not really interested in medicine as a whole, but he *was* interested in physiology and psychology. When he was invited to teach at Harvard Medical School, he offered, in 1875, the first American course in experimental psychology. As a result, he eventually transferred to the philosophy department, to which the discipline of psychology was at that time assigned.

William James's bent was philosophical and ultimately religious. He was also cosmopolitan, witty and human—in almost every respect the temperamental opposite of Wundt. He made Harvard an important center for the study of psychology. His great book, *The Principles of Psychology*, published in 1890, is still in use.

James did not dream of confining his work to the experimental method. He found the Germanic tradition of looking for elements of sensation tedious to an extreme. He once wrote of Fechner, "It would be terrible if even such a dear old man as this could saddle our Science forever with his patient whimsies, and, in a world so full of more nutritious objects of attention, compel all future students to plough through the difficulties . . . of his . . . works." He despaired of ever pinning down Wundt's theories: "Cut him up like a worm and each fragment crawls."

James described consciousness as both continuous and selective. He likened it to the life of a bird, now swooping in motion, now perching on an object. To him the element of consciousness that was responsible for selection—for adjustment to the environment—was far more interesting than its ability to concentrate on the sound of a metronome in a laboratory.

During this same period in Vienna, Sigmund Freud was writing detailed case histories of emotionally disturbed patients. He was trying to show that their repressed, or unconscious, sexual desires exercised a powerful influence on their conscious behavior. Freud was a physician, and his exhaustive analysis of the unconscious was developed outside the field of psychology. Nevertheless, his conclusions on the enormous importance of the unconscious influenced psychology—and indeed, all of the thinking of the Western world.

A momentous quarter of a century

Wundt's first great book, *Principles of Physiological Psychology*, was published in 1874. Freud's *Interpretation of Dreams* appeared in 1900. In the intervening period, little more than a quarter of a century, a psychologist-philosopher—William James—had eloquently warned that consciousness could not be caged for study, and a physician—Sigmund Freud—had opened up the subtle world of dreams and sex. Both had used insight rather than experimental methods. But both were also trained scientists. Their approach to conclusions was disciplined and quite different from those of the ancient philosophers. And both concluded that man's entire mental life was a very complicated process indeed.

By the 1910s two major schools of experimental psychology broke free from Wundt's absorption in the minutiae of sensation. They developed simultaneously, in opposition to Wundt and to each other. One was the school of behaviorism, launched in 1913 by an American, John B. Watson. The other was the German *Gestalt* school. Watson declared, in brief, that the whole business of introspection—Wundt's basic method —was unreliable, unscientific and suspect. The only reliable thing a scientist could deal with was outward behavior. Watson's ideas stimulated American psychologists enormously. They began to study in their laboratories what stimulus produced what response and, above all, what stimuli produced what changes in behavior. They began to enter many of the fields associated with psychology today—education, child-raising, treatment of the mentally ill. And in doing so they left Wundt far behind.

Experiments with a toy

Experimental psychology received still another impetus on a summer day in 1910. A young psychologist named Max Wertheimer was aboard a train to the Rhineland for a vacation when he was suddenly struck with an inspiration that led him to get off the train at Frankfurt. There he went to a toy store and bought a stroboscope, then asked to borrow a little space at the University of Frankfurt for his experiments—and stayed on six years. A toy stroboscope is a device to show a series of still pictures in rapid succession, thus giving the illusion of movement.

On the train Wertheimer had been speculating about the phenomenon that had puzzled psychologists for some time: that man thought he saw motion when two similar objects appeared in quick succession. The most obvious example, of course, is the appearance of motion given by a succession of discrete photographs that make up motion picture frames, which we see as "moving pictures." A similar effect can be achieved by placing two lights side by side in a dark room, switching them off and on alternately. To the observer, one light seems to dance back and forth. To Wertheimer these phenomena, and the effects produced by the toy stroboscope, were convincing proof that sensation alone could not account for our perception of motion; he was sure that something more than the five senses was involved in perception. This was a hypothesis that struck at the roots of ideas prevalent since the days of John Locke, and particularly at all of Wundt's work.

For the next 30 years, Wertheimer and two colleagues, Wolfgang Köhler and Kurt Koffka, were the principal spokesmen for what became known as the Gestalt school of psychology. *Gestalt,* which means "shape" or "form," has come in psychological terminology to mean "whole." The Gestalt experiments were designed to prove that perception is a more extraordinary phenomenon than the combination of separate elements of sensation. They argued, rather, that perception operates, so to speak, in reverse: we tend to perceive a whole configuration first, and then the separate elements.

The Gestalt school believed that immediate, meaningful perception is arrived at by the mental ability to create relationships. A song is recognized by learning its melody, not by learning a succession of individual notes. Furthermore, a song is recognized in different keys, a fact that proves that the relationships of the notes are more important than the individual notes themselves.

Gestalt doctrines were slow to gain acceptance in the U.S. at first, for behaviorism was dominant, and Gestalt theories seemed to offer few possibilities of immediate application. But since the 1940s the old battle lines have been melting away. Behaviorists and Gestalt psychologists listen to and benefit from one another's conclusions. Nevertheless, the behaviorists and the Gestalt school still represent two basically different approaches to the mind. Many psychologists, particularly in America, still prefer to study behavior, believing that man's outward acts can be more accurately observed, and are possibly more vitally significant, than what goes on inside his head. Others, known as cognitive psychologists, are still fascinated by man's inner mental processes. Many are still studying the original problem posed by Wertheimer: how does the mind perceive? But their careful reconstructions of how man organizes masses of material in order to understand his world have led them to a vastly more interesting mind than the "blotter for sensations" that Wundt studied. It has led them to the higher processes of learning, remembering and thinking.

The behaviorists and the cognitive school together have led psychology away from Wundt's Leipzig laboratory in directions William James would have approved: toward the world in which we act and detect meaning. Nevertheless, psychology owes a debt to Wundt, and most psychologists speak more kindly of him than James did. He staked out its province—the whole of mental life as described by Descartes—and insisted that the discipline of psychology arm itself with its own experimental techniques.

"An animal who thinks"

Since Wundt's day, using his techniques and methods, psychology has extended its field of investigation far from pure sensation. In the course of doing so, it has begun to identify a whole range of mental functions very similar to those on which man based his first claims of superiority over other animals. Two thousand years ago the Roman statesman-philosopher Lucius Annaeus Seneca declared, "Man is an animal who thinks." Now psychologists ask, "What *is* thinking?" Obviously thinking has something to do with consciousness, since we do not think (at least not in the popular sense of the word) when we are unconscious. This raises another unresolved question: what is the nature of consciousness?

Memory and learning raise similar difficulties. Animals can learn a

CHOICE IN BROWN AND WHITE
The drawing above is among many designed by Gestalt psychologists to demonstrate that the individual organizes visual sensations into perceptions. The simple brown and white pattern can be organized in two ways, and the viewer does both, alternately perceiving a white goblet against a brown ground or two silhouettes against a white ground.

great deal. The behavior of some higher animals shows that they use the memory of what they have learned to help solve problems later on.

Thinking, consciousness, memory and learning—these are all different terms to signify that mental life includes meaning, understanding. Here man's superiority over animals becomes apparent. Once we understand a concept, we can generalize. We can recall it again and again, as we do in memory. We can make predictions from it, as we do in imagination.

The best hope of obtaining a full understanding of these mental processes lies in the use of new techniques still in the course of development. Many sciences have played a part in exploring the workings of the mind. Anatomists and physiologists have shown us the detailed structure of the nervous system and the means by which it functions. Physicians have studied the effects of damage and disease, and have drawn conclusions about the normal mind from their observations of the abnormal. Psychologists have carried out experiments on behavior and perception in man and animals, and psychoanalysts have directed their investigations into the dark world of the unconscious. Computers have been designed to imitate, as far as possible, human thought processes, and this technique has already taught us something about learning and memory. When more complex machines are devised, they may teach us more about more sophisticated functions of this fascinating factor of life.

The Instrument
of the
Nervous System

Man's nervous system is awesomely complex. Networks of nerve cells, some with fibers several feet long, run throughout the body, connecting every distant bit of tissue with the 10 billion nerve cells of the governing brain. Electrical impulses travel along these pathways at speeds ranging from two to 200 miles an hour, leaping across narrow gaps between cells, relaying intelligence to and from the brain. This essay shows the system at work during the complicated act of playing the piano, when the various networks perform a dazzling array of tasks simultaneously. The heart beats, the lungs draw breath, the metabolism of the body is maintained. The data of the senses are coordinated, memories called up, scores of muscles precisely directed, emotions acted on and thoughts conceived. Only a nervous system as elaborate as man's makes possible his more demanding physical and intellectual activities—such as playing the piano.

ROUTES FOR MUSICAL MESSAGES
The picture on the opposite page is a photograph of a pianist. On it have been sketched the two hemispheres of the brain, a network of nerves throughout the arms, and a connecting length of spinal cord. This system of billions of cells and miles of fibers can relay many messages at once. The player is a composer-pianist, John Cooper, pictures of whom are used throughout this essay.

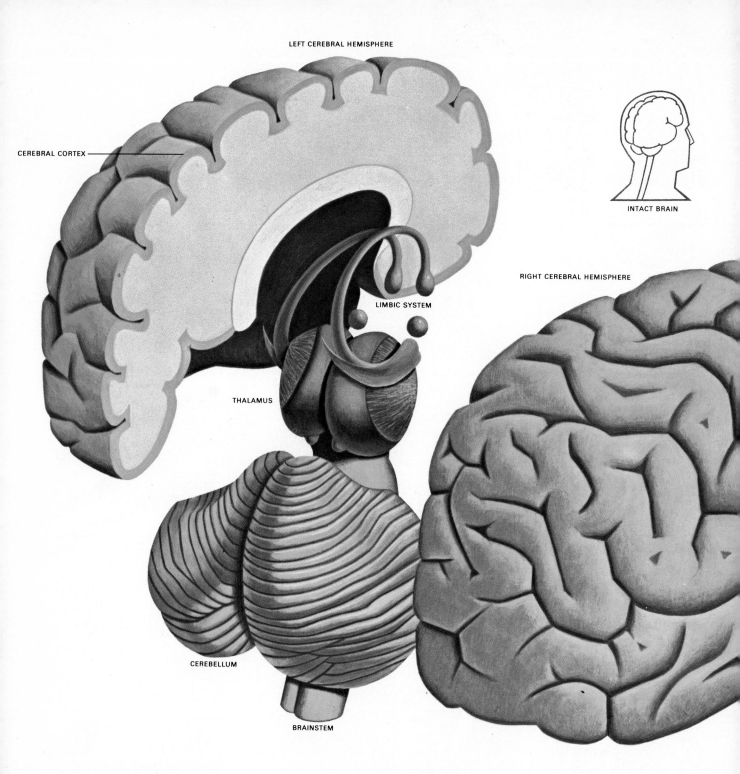

LEFT CEREBRAL HEMISPHERE

CEREBRAL CORTEX

INTACT BRAIN

RIGHT CEREBRAL HEMISPHERE

LIMBIC SYSTEM

THALAMUS

CEREBELLUM

BRAINSTEM

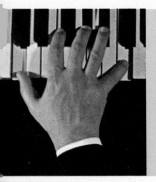

MUSCULAR COORDINATION
Each of the four colored brain areas in the drawing above performs a different task. The cerebellum and brainstem work below the level of consciousness. They keep the higher brain centers, chiefly the cerebral cortex, informed on the condition of the muscles, and modify unrealistic demands on them. The muscles of the pianist's hand are smoothly coordinated with their help.

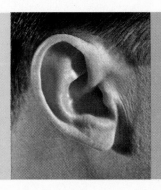

SENSE INTEGRATION
Messages from eyes, ears and other receivers lead through the thalamus. The thalamus and cortex together are the centers that integrate incoming sense data, so that the sound of music combines with the touch of the keys into one experience. Auditory nerve impulses enter two small protuberances at the bases of the thalamus, which are shown in the drawing above.

The Great Knot inside the Skull

The 10 billion nerve cells of the brain make a bumpy knot of gray and white matter inside the skull. Careful investigation has revealed a number of groupings of these cells. One possible way of dividing them is illustrated in the four different colors in the large drawing at left.

Some of the groupings are visible as anatomical entities. The two cerebral hemispheres, for example, are the largest single unit of the nervous system. Each consists of a core of connecting fibers covered with a layer of gray matter, called the cortex. The thalamus and the cerebellum are also paired bodies. The limbic system, deep within the brain, is not so readily seen as an anatomical unit, but research has identified it as an area which affects specific functions.

The brain is an integrated unit, with many connecting nerve cells. Nevertheless, some parts seem to be more directly involved in some functions than other parts. The four captions at the bottom of these pages, each color-keyed to one of the areas shown at left, describe the functions associated with each area. The area most thoroughly investigated, the cortex, is mapped in detail at right.

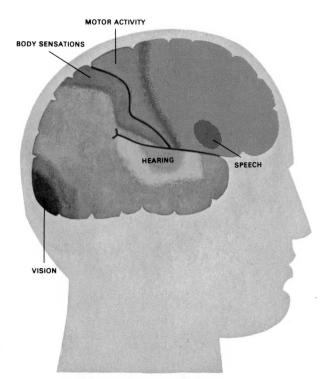

A MAP OF CONSCIOUSNESS
The thick, convoluted cortex, or covering, of the two cerebral hemispheres governs man's most complicated conscious functions. Sense data are received here and voluntary muscular activity is initiated here. By artificially stimulating the cortex at various points, scientists have been able to map specific areas of its surface related to specific sensory and motor functions.

THOUGHT AND MEMORY
The cerebral cortex is the brain's most elaborate center, where sensations are registered and voluntary actions are initiated. It has been called "the seat of all which is exclusively human in the mind," for here decisions are made, higher thought processes occur, and memories are stored. It is in use as the pianist reads a score or recalls thousands of memorized notes.

EMOTIONS
The limbic system contributes to emotions, such as those aroused by playing or listening to music. Experiments on animals have demonstrated the importance of this system buried deep in the brain to emotional reactions. Fear and fearlessness, hunger and satiety, rage and sexual urges have been aroused in laboratory animals by stimulating it with electrodes in various places.

Well Nourished and Well Protected

The soft mass of the adult brain is perfectly motionless. It does not contract, divide or grow—yet it consumes up to 25 per cent of the blood's oxygen supply. This poses a puzzle, for everywhere else in the body the amount of oxygen used is directly related to measurable physical work performed. For example, when a man plays the piano, the blood steps up its flow into the muscles of his fingers and arms, bringing food and oxygen for conversion into immediate energy. The brain, comprising only 2 per cent of the body's weight, is constantly bathed in blood—its vessels receive 20 per cent of all the blood that streams from the heart. If the flow is interrupted for only 15 seconds, loss of consciousness results; an interruption of four minutes causes irreversible damage to most cerebral cells. Evidently great amounts of energy are consumed in the production of mental life, but exactly how is not known.

The brain is extraordinarily delicate, and is provided with extraordinary protection. The four arteries that feed it have an elaborate system of intercommunication, so that if one or even two arteries are blocked, blood can be rerouted through the others. It is swaddled in three distinct protective layers—more than any other organ of the body. Like the fetus, it swims in a surrounding fluid that absorbs shocks. Jellylike tissue, blood vessels and fluid are all encased in a tough membrane. Finally, the whole is surrounded by the bone of the skull.

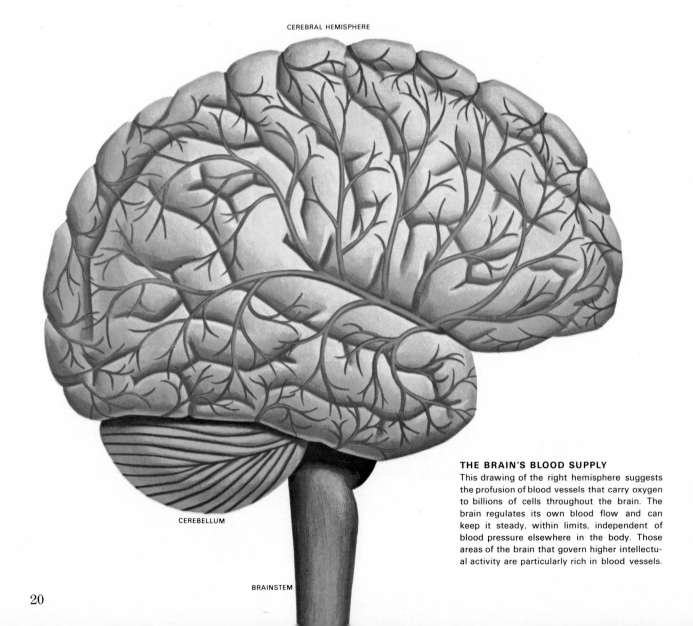

CEREBRAL HEMISPHERE

CEREBELLUM

BRAINSTEM

THE BRAIN'S BLOOD SUPPLY

This drawing of the right hemisphere suggests the profusion of blood vessels that carry oxygen to billions of cells throughout the brain. The brain regulates its own blood flow and can keep it steady, within limits, independent of blood pressure elsewhere in the body. Those areas of the brain that govern higher intellectual activity are particularly rich in blood vessels.

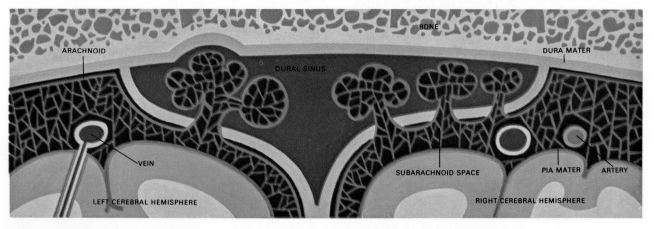

ARACHNOID • BONE • DURA MATER • DURAL SINUS • VEIN • SUBARACHNOID SPACE • PIA MATER • ARTERY • LEFT CEREBRAL HEMISPHERE • RIGHT CEREBRAL HEMISPHERE

SHIELD UPON SHIELD

The brain's protective layers are drawn here in a cross section of the forehead. The outer layer is the cranial bone *(top)*. Underneath it is the dura mater (Latin for "hard mother"), a tough membrane which enfolds both hemispheres. Next comes the arachnoid (Greek for "cobweb"), an elastic membrane that encloses the subarachnoid space. This space is filled with filaments, blood vessels and cerebrospinal fluid, described in the diagram below. The final layer is a thin membrane, the pia mater ("gentle mother"), that hugs the cortex in all its convolutions.

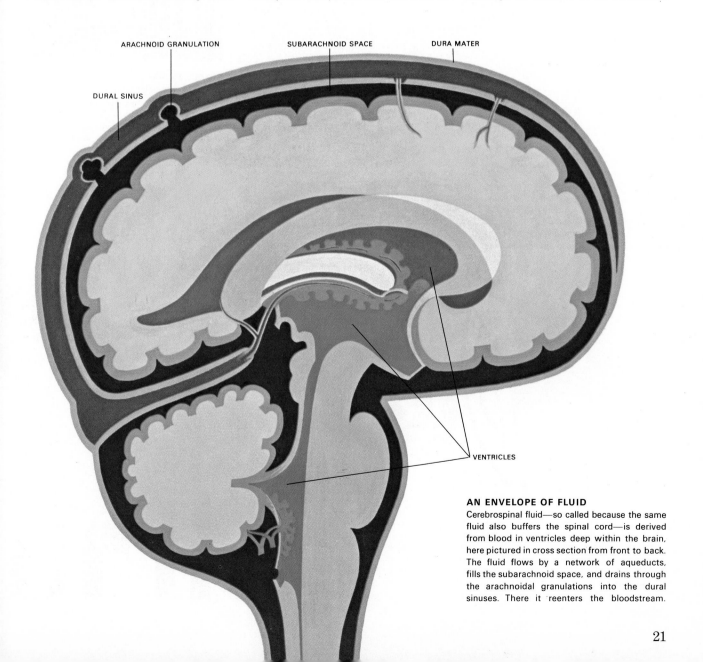

ARACHNOID GRANULATION • SUBARACHNOID SPACE • DURA MATER • DURAL SINUS • VENTRICLES

AN ENVELOPE OF FLUID

Cerebrospinal fluid—so called because the same fluid also buffers the spinal cord—is derived from blood in ventricles deep within the brain, here pictured in cross section from front to back. The fluid flows by a network of aqueducts, fills the subarachnoid space, and drains through the arachnoidal granulations into the dural sinuses. There it reenters the bloodstream.

THE AUDITORY SYSTEM

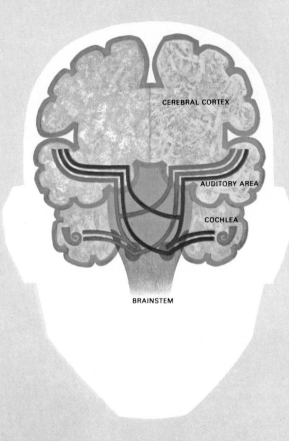

CEREBRAL CORTEX

AUDITORY AREA

COCHLEA

BRAINSTEM

GIFTED THUMBS

Each of the pianist's fingers is controlled by a specific area in the cerebral cortex on the opposite side of his brain. Relatively large segments of the cortex are given to man's hands, and the extra-flexible thumbs, in turn, are controlled by larger areas than the other fingers.

CIRCUITOUS ROUTING

Nerve impulses originated by musical notes travel to the cortex by more than one route, there to be registered according to their frequency, or pitch. Some of the paths these impulses take cross to the opposite side of the brain in the brainstem, at relay stations like the two indicated in the picture above by the oval spots. Other paths cross over higher up, at other relay stations, and some do not cross at all. Thus, although more of the impulses end in the opposite side of the cortex, some of them are registered in both cerebral hemispheres.

COCHLEA   MIDDLE EAR

COCHLEA

AN EAR FOR AIR WAVES

The snail-shaped cochlea is the ear's organ for sorting notes of different frequencies. Vibrations created by a musical note enter the middle ear and eventually reach tiny hairs in the cochlea. A stylized drawing of the cochlea is on the right above. Its color is graduated because lower frequencies stimulate hairs deep inside, while higher frequencies stimulate the hairs nearer the entrance. The movements of the hairs in turn activate chains of nerve cells—the auditory paths shown in the drawing at the top of the page—all of which end in the cortex.

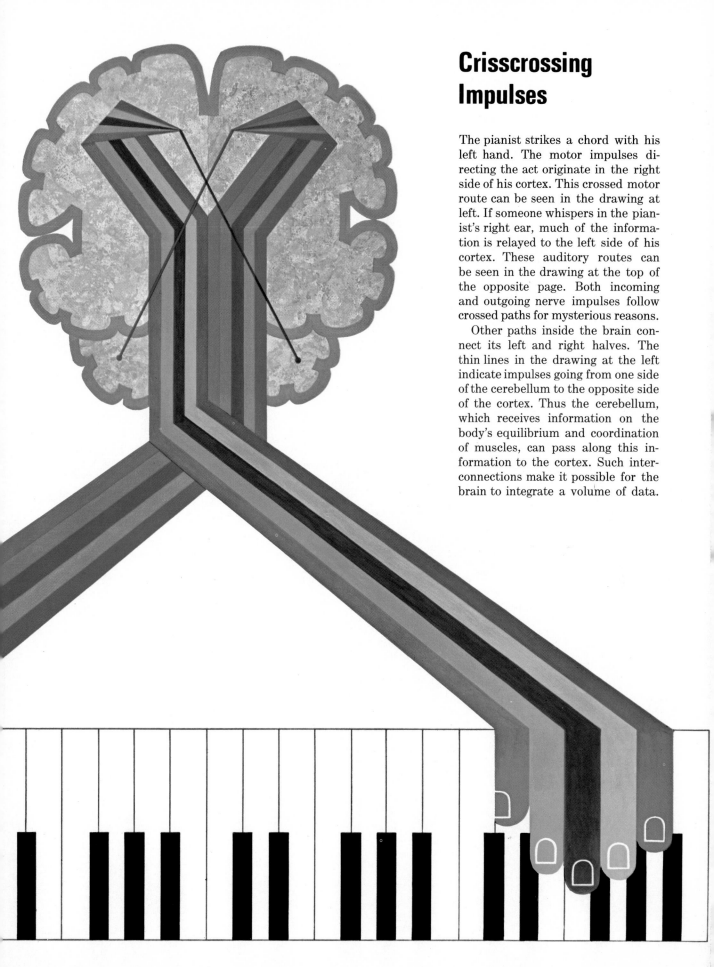

Crisscrossing Impulses

The pianist strikes a chord with his left hand. The motor impulses directing the act originate in the right side of his cortex. This crossed motor route can be seen in the drawing at left. If someone whispers in the pianist's right ear, much of the information is relayed to the left side of his cortex. These auditory routes can be seen in the drawing at the top of the opposite page. Both incoming and outgoing nerve impulses follow crossed paths for mysterious reasons.

Other paths inside the brain connect its left and right halves. The thin lines in the drawing at the left indicate impulses going from one side of the cerebellum to the opposite side of the cortex. Thus the cerebellum, which receives information on the body's equilibrium and coordination of muscles, can pass along this information to the cortex. Such interconnections make it possible for the brain to integrate a volume of data.

THE SPINAL NERVES

The human torso, the arms and the legs are served by 31 pairs of great spinal nerves rooted to either side of the spinal cord, which branch out into ever-finer subdivisions until their tips are single fibers. The painting at right shows a few of these subdivisions. A pianist's directions to his fingers, for example, would proceed from his cortex, down the spinal cord, out a spinal nerve to a network near the shoulder, where directions for each finger would be sent along the appropriate subsidiary nerve. Some would enter the arm's radial nerve, some its median nerve and some its ulnar nerve. Other fibers in these nerves carry sensory impulses, which follow the same routes in reverse.

Each of the nerves following the ribs in the painting represents a similar subdividing distribution system.

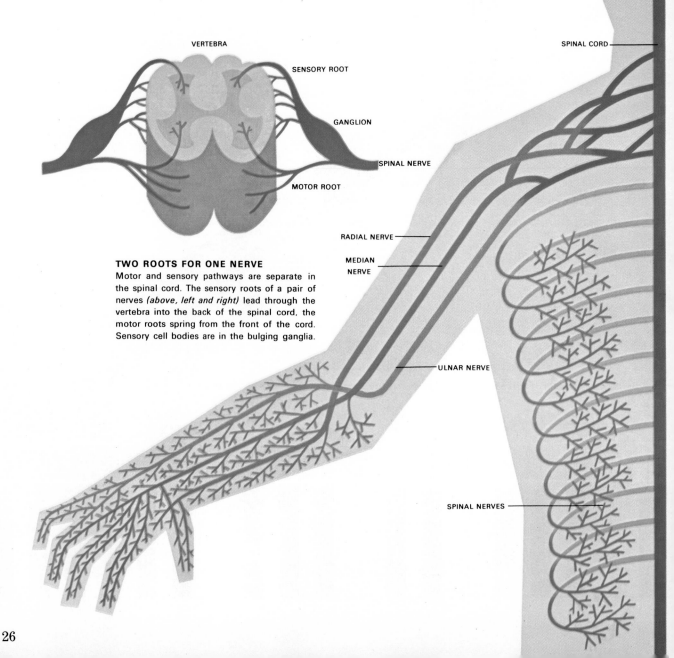

BRAIN

SPINAL CORD

VERTEBRA

SENSORY ROOT

GANGLION

SPINAL NERVE

MOTOR ROOT

RADIAL NERVE

MEDIAN NERVE

ULNAR NERVE

SPINAL NERVES

TWO ROOTS FOR ONE NERVE
Motor and sensory pathways are separate in the spinal cord. The sensory roots of a pair of nerves *(above, left and right)* lead through the vertebra into the back of the spinal cord, the motor roots spring from the front of the cord. Sensory cell bodies are in the bulging ganglia.

The Peripheral Nervous System

TWO-LANE HIGHWAYS

The time exposure on the preceding foldout pages, made by putting lights on pianist Cooper's hands, symbolizes the enormous number of messages that must fly between his hands and brain in order for him to play. Such messages travel along the network of nerves, called the peripheral system, that connects the brain and spinal cord to all parts of the body.

Each color area in the painting at right, for example, represents an area of skin served by one of the great spinal or cranial nerves. These nerves are composed of thousands of fibers, each capable of carrying a separate message. The fibers of sensory nerve cells carry sense data from skin, muscles and bone to the brain; the fibers of motor nerve cells carry the brain's orders to muscles and organs. Most nerves contain both kinds of fibers.

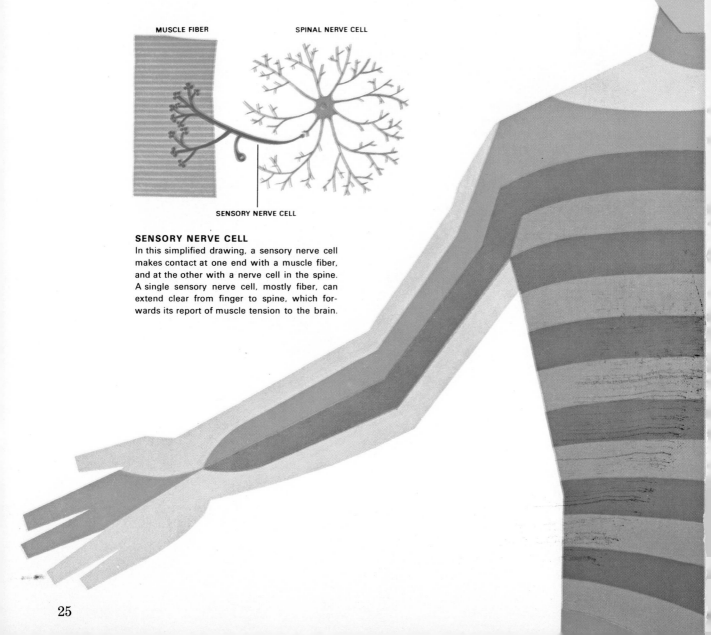

MUSCLE FIBER SPINAL NERVE CELL

SENSORY NERVE CELL

SENSORY NERVE CELL
In this simplified drawing, a sensory nerve cell makes contact at one end with a muscle fiber, and at the other with a nerve cell in the spine. A single sensory nerve cell, mostly fiber, can extend clear from finger to spine, which forwards its report of muscle tension to the brain.

THE INTERNAL ORGANS

The autonomic system of nerves relays the vital orders that keep the body in good working order. It regulates the organs and blood vessels shown in the painting at left, and others, affecting circulation, respiration and metabolism. The sympathetic nerve system tends to tense and constrict involuntary muscles and blood vessels and step up the activity of glands. It is most clearly seen in the body's swift reaction to emergencies. In the "fight or flight" reaction, the stomach tightens, blood pressure increases and adrenalin pours into the system.

The parasympathetic system in many ways works in antithesis to the sympathetic, tending to slow and relax the same organs. Together, both systems enable the organs to work smoothly, yet adapt quickly to change.

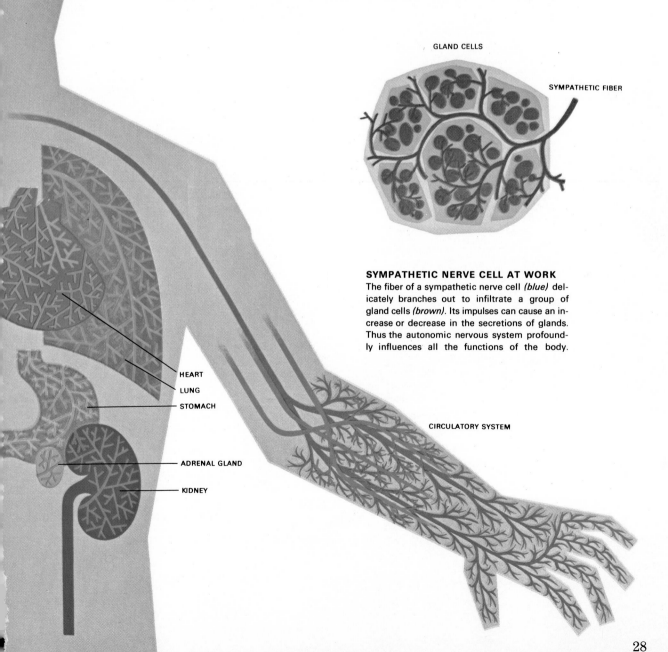

GLAND CELLS

SYMPATHETIC FIBER

SYMPATHETIC NERVE CELL AT WORK
The fiber of a sympathetic nerve cell *(blue)* delicately branches out to infiltrate a group of gland cells *(brown)*. Its impulses can cause an increase or decrease in the secretions of glands. Thus the autonomic nervous system profoundly influences all the functions of the body.

CIRCULATORY SYSTEM

HEART
LUNG
STOMACH

ADRENAL GLAND

KIDNEY

THE AUTONOMIC NERVES

Besides the network of motor nerve cells that direct voluntary activity, an altogether different network of motor nerve cells connects the brain with internal organs, the circulatory system and mucous membranes. This is called the autonomic system, because it works automatically, requiring no conscious commands.

The painting at left indicates two subsystems of nerves within the system: the sympathetic and the parasympathetic. The sympathetic *(blue)* is more pervasive, and has two chains of ganglia, called sympathetic trunks, on either side of the spine *(green)*. The large vagus nerve *(orange)* belongs to the parasympathetic system. It has endings in the throat that control swallowing, and other endings in the major organs that are shown in the painting on the following page.

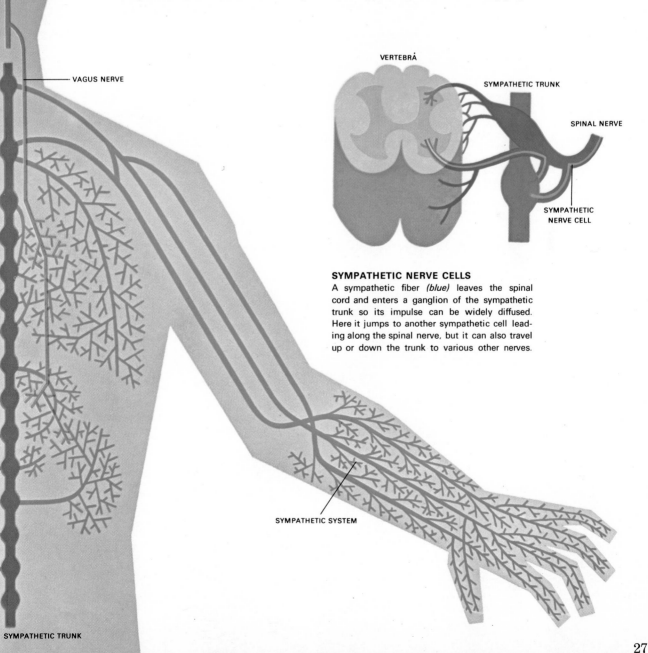

VERTEBRA

SYMPATHETIC TRUNK

SPINAL NERVE

SYMPATHETIC NERVE CELL

VAGUS NERVE

SYMPATHETIC SYSTEM

SYMPATHETIC TRUNK

SYMPATHETIC NERVE CELLS

A sympathetic fiber *(blue)* leaves the spinal cord and enters a ganglion of the sympathetic trunk so its impulse can be widely diffused. Here it jumps to another sympathetic cell leading along the spinal nerve, but it can also travel up or down the trunk to various other nerves.

2

Mechanisms
of
Mentality

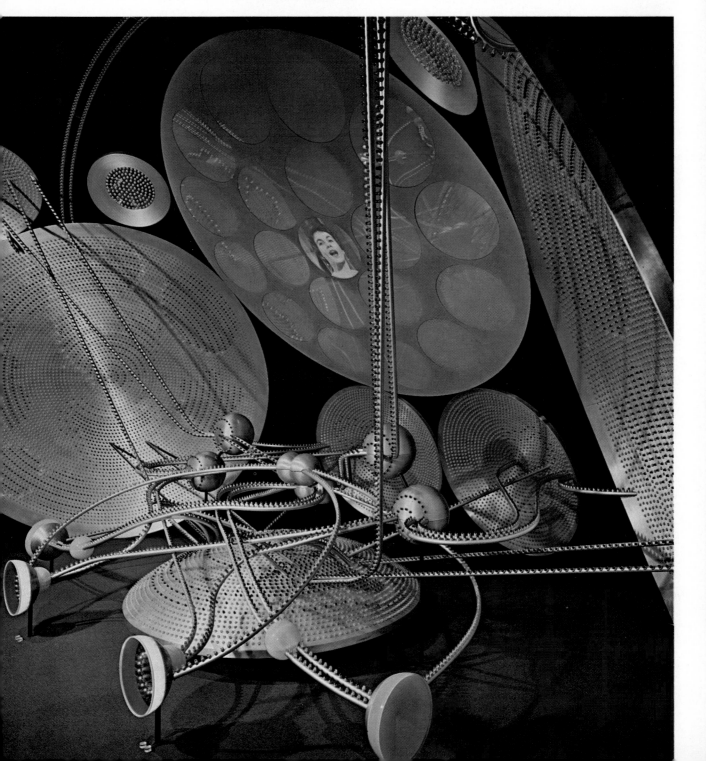

WHATEVER THE NATURE OF THE MIND, there is no doubt that the mechanism through which it works is the nervous system. Unimaginably tiny events occur among the cells of nervous tissue, and a broad range of processes takes place: responses to sensory stimuli, voluntary and involuntary body movements, conscious and unconscious thinking. Something happens inside the nervous system when we take a walk or add up a column of figures in our head. It follows that examination of how the mind functions must begin with the nervous system.

Although the activity of human nerve cells produces a great variety of effects, the cells are similar in structure. A nerve cell has three components: the cell body; a number of fibers, called dendrites, which can pick up electrical impulses from neighboring cells; and a single fiber, or axon, which can pass on impulses to other cells. With a few exceptions, nerve cells are elaborate chemical devices designed to conduct impulses in one direction only: from the tips of the dendrites into the cell body, and then from the cell body out along the axon, which usually terminates among a dendrite cluster of other cells.

The nerve cells of the human body are gathered into three great structures that comprise the nervous system. First and foremost is the brain, a mass of tissue inside the skull that consists of about 10 billion interconnected nerve cells. Stemming from the brain is the spinal cord, a sheath of nervous tissue enclosed in membranes, extending two thirds of the way down the backbone. The central core of this sheath is H-shaped and is made up of nerve cells; the surrounding matter is for the most part long cables of fibers, for the axons of spinal nerve cells may extend two or three feet.

The brain and the cord are the two structures that make up the central nervous system.

The third structure of the nervous system as a whole is a network of nerves reaching throughout the body called the peripheral system. The main trunk lines consist of cell fibers emerging from the brain and cord, bundled together into large cranial and spinal nerves. Each bundle is a cable composed of many thousands of fibers. These nerves divide and subdivide again and again so that, finally, single minute fibers reach into every area of the body. The peripheral system and the spinal cord together provide physical routes of communication, most of which can be seen with the naked eye, between every part of the body and the brain.

But to say that the nervous system is physical is far from saying that it is simple. Its workings are so complex, its effects so various that we are only beginning to understand its processes. Moreover, it is sealed inside the living body; our knowledge of it has had to be painstakingly acquired over the centuries from the work of many men.

Some of the first experiments on the nervous system were carried out

DISKS, CABLES AND A BRUNETTE
The awesome assembly of disks and cables on the opposite page, designed for a medical convention, represents a human brain and outlying sense organs. When the eyes (blue bowls, *lower left*) see an object, red lights flash along the cables to brain centers (large disks, *left and right*), and the consciousness screen *(center)* records the vision—in this case a brunette.

31

by the Greek physician Galen in the second century after Christ. One of the great neurologists of all time, Galen found seven of the 12 major nerves in the head, or cranial nerves, by performing postmortems. He theorized that the nerves were hollow, and that "animal spirits," flowing through them from the brain, produced sensation, movement and thought. This was an ingenious guess, and in the absence of any knowledge of electricity, it constituted a remarkably accurate one. Galen also explored nerve routes between the brain and the rest of the body. By severing the spinal cords of animals in various places, he found that nerves that controlled breathing were connected to the cord at a point closer to the brain than those controlling simple body movements. A cut low in the neck paralyzed most of the body, but only a high cut paralyzed the diaphragm so that the animal could no longer breathe.

"Here are my books"

During the Middle Ages physiological research languished and neurological knowledge remained for 1,400 years more or less where Galen had left it. The Renaissance saw a vigorous reawakening of interest in scientific matters, one result being William Harvey's demonstration in the 17th Century of the circulation of the blood. Nevertheless, when Harvey's contemporary, the French philosopher and mathematician René Descartes tried to explain motion and sensation, he fell back on Galen's theories of animal spirits and hollow nerves. There were few texts on the nervous system, and Descartes dissected animals in an endeavor to see how they functioned. (He once pointed to his dissections and said to a visitor, "Here are my books.") He wrote a detailed theory on body movement, called *Traité de l'Homme*, in which he compared the body's mechanisms to those of the life-sized mechanical dolls which had become all the rage among the rich of the time.

Descartes' book described the elaborate dolls placed about the fountains and grottoes of Louis XIII's Royal Gardens. They were operated by hydraulic mechanisms, a fact which gave him a ready analogy to fluid animal spirits. The dolls walked, played musical instruments and even appeared to speak. Descartes was particularly fascinated by a figure of Diana bathing in a pool. If a visitor drew close to watch, he stepped on a tile, and Diana disappeared behind rose bushes. If the visitor tried to follow, he stepped on another tile, and a figure of Neptune appeared, barring the way with his trident. Descartes acquired a doll of his own, which he called *Ma Fille Franchina* (My Daughter Franchina). According to one story, he took Franchina with him on a sea voyage. The captain, seeing a large doll walking his deck, threw it overboard, certain that such lifelike machinery must be the work of the devil.

Descartes' explanations of motion on a mechanistic basis hardly

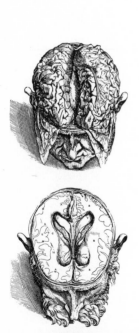

THE BRAIN EXPOSED

These drawings are from *De Humani Corporis Fabrica*, the work of the famous 16th Century anatomist Andreas Vesalius that is often called the cornerstone of modern anatomy. At top is the brain after the outer membrane has been removed. The brain at center is sliced longitudinally, the one at bottom partially scooped out, revealing the cerebellum. Vesalius worked from real models: "the heads of executed criminals . . . still warm."

illuminated the field of neurology, but he performed one valuable service that influenced later research: he described for the first time certain involuntary responses the body makes to certain stimuli, the kind of response that later came to be termed a "reflex." The best-known reflex is the jerk of the leg when a knee tendon is tapped. Another is the blink of the eyes at an unexpected flash of light.

Explaining the riddle of the reflex action was the first great milestone in the development of modern neurological knowledge. An early clue was discovered in 1811, when an English surgeon, Sir Charles Bell, determined that the nerve cell fibers entering the spinal cord were divided by function into two distinct types. The fibers at the back of the cord were routes for nerve impulses coming from sense receptors to the brain; those at the front of the cord were routes for nerve impulses from the brain to muscles and organs. Eleven years later, a French physiologist, François Magendie, independently made the same discovery without knowing of Bell's work. (Magendie's experiments were even more conclusive than Sir Charles's, and today their joint discovery is known as the Bell-Magendie law.) Sir Charles's subsequent work led to another law: that nerve cells can normally carry impulses in only one direction. The knowledge that half our spinal nerve cells send impulses in one direction, half in the other, began to make intelligible the complicated system of nerve fibers in animals and man. Sir Charles also showed that some nerves are entirely sensory, because all their fibers lead into the central nervous system; others are entirely motor, because all their fibers lead from the central nervous system; most are sheaths containing both kinds of fibers.

Research into the deceptively simple reflex action culminated in its current explanation by Sir Charles Sherrington, a physiologist at Oxford whose long life spanned from 1857 to 1952. His work cast a flood of light on the functions of the nerve cell, the spinal cord and ultimately the entire nervous system. For this he became a co-winner of the Nobel Prize in 1932. Sherrington worked on the so-called scratch reflex that is familiar to every dog-owner. If a dog's back is rubbed, it will lift a hind leg and scratch. Sherrington traced the route of the dog's nerve impulses from the sensory receptors, or fiber tips, in the dog's back. He followed them along the sensory fibers to the spinal cord, across connections to motor fibers, and thence outward again to the responding muscles.

The simplest electrical circuit

This arc from sensory nerve cell through the spinal cord to motor nerve cell is the simplest electrical circuit in the nervous system. Circuits involving stimulus and response must go through the central nervous system at some point, where the impulse is passed from a sensory to a motor

"ANIMAL SPIRITS" MOVE A FOOT
Taken from René Descartes' book *Traité de l'Homme,* this 1664 wood engraving illustrates his theory of the workings of reflex action. The long fiber running from the foot to a cranial cavity is "pulled" by the fire's heat. The tug releases "animal spirits" in the cavity. The fluid spirits rush to muscles throughout the body. The head turns, the hand reaches toward the painful foot and the foot is yanked away from the fire.

cell. Many circuits in lower animals and the handful in man called the simple reflexes go no higher than the spinal cord. For example, when the spinal cord in a lower animal like a frog is severed near the brain, it will still reflexively lift its hind foot to scratch if its side is irritated, though it has no awareness of doing so, for no message reaches its brain.

An understanding of the simple reflex arc provided the first clear picture of the nervous system as a pattern of circuits. However, it yields only an inkling of the system's complexity, and physiologists still face many fascinating unknowns. For one thing, most of man's nerve activity involves circuits leading through the billions of cells of the brain, where innumerable interconnections offer many choices in the responses made. Unfortunately the circuits cannot be easily traced in the brain. The elaborate chemistry of the nerve fibers has been studied in detail and a good bit is known about the chemical processes that keep an impulse moving along its path. But there are still questions on how nerve cells convert energy into impulses initially. It is known that sensory nerve cells are extraordinarily sensitive to energy, and can convert the most minute amounts of it into impulses. For example, one light quantum—the smallest unit of radiant energy—may be enough to stimulate one sensory cell in the retina. It is impossible for anything to be more sensitive to light than this. If the human ear were any more sensitive than it is, the noise of colliding air molecules would mask many of the sounds we want to hear. The olfactory nerve cells detect mercaptan, a sulphur compound, in a ratio of one part to 50 billion parts of air. Sensory nerve cells respond to external stimuli that can be measured, but little is known about the initiation of motor and other impulses in the brain.

What is consciousness?

Perhaps the most challenging of all the unknowns is how these electro-chemical impulses can produce such an astonishing variety of effects, ranging from dreaming to reciting a poem to writing a letter. Psychologists have wrestled with categories for them, such as conscious- versus unconscious-mental activity and voluntary- versus involuntary-motor activity. But nerve activities cannot be isolated in tight compartments. In practice, all our nervous processes are so highly integrated that hatches simply refuse to close between them. As a result, the very word "consciousness" is one of the most difficult psychologists have to define.

Some of the complicated nerve circuits clearly carry incoming sensory information that reaches our consciousness. We feel, for example, the touch of a feather on the skin. Other circuits then relay conscious directions from the brain to distant muscles: we brush the feather away.

It is equally clear that some circuits operate below the level of consciousness. Most of the motor impulses that control our visceral organs and keep us functioning properly are unconscious. Happily, a separate network of motor nerve cells, called the autonomic system, carries on this activity, regulating body temperature, blood pressure, rate of digestion, etc., according to changing requirements. Impulses starting in the brain or spinal cord go out along two subsystems of autonomic motor nerves: the sympathetic and the parasympathetic. They activate viscera and glands, and cause veins and arteries to dilate and contract. The impulses are exactly the same as those that produce voluntary movements.

A report on nausea

The viscera may function unconsciously, but sensory nerves can keep the consciousness closely informed as to their state. When everything is functioning properly, we are unaware that anything is going on. But a bout of nausea reported by sensory nerves becomes uppermost in the consciousness. Similarly, our conscious life profoundly affects the autonomic system. We would be strongly conscious of a lion if we should happen to meet one around the corner, and a message would be relayed to the autonomic system which is responsible for the body's swift, automatic and highly practical adjustments in the face of danger. The autonomic system would spring into action, sending messages to the heart and vascular system, the respiratory system, the digestive organs, the adrenal gland and even to the hair on the back of the head. The heart would pump faster, the bronchial passages would dilate, more blood would be dispatched to muscles, and increased amounts of adrenalin would be secreted into the blood system. (The rising of the hair is probably a vestigial remnant of a reaction designed to make a frightened person look larger or more alarming.) The other reactions are preparations for a violent expenditure of energy in either doing battle or running away.

These "fight or flight" reactions, as psychologists describe them, turn up in moderate degrees upon receipt of all kinds of messages from the conscious. Most people cannot even tell a lie without stepping up the autonomic activity of the sweat glands, the respiratory system and the heart: measuring changes in rates of perspiration, breathing and heartbeat is what a lie detector does. On many other occasions, appropriate or inappropriate, we have "butterflies" in the stomach, clammy hands, pounding heart, a flush or loss of color.

The diseases frequently diagnosed as psychosomatic, or mental, in origin are further proof that conscious nervous activity and autonomic activity work hand in hand. Chronic tension can lead to physical disorders such as peptic ulcers and migraine headaches. Nerve circuits that serve our conscious mental life can also affect the autonomic system. A child in difficulties at school may be sick every morning at eight o'clock. The child's wish to be ill in order to skip school and the

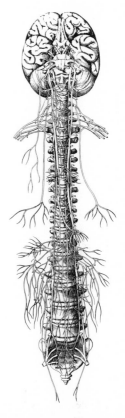

A LACY TRACERY OF NERVES
A remarkably accurate picture of the sympathetic nervous system, this is based on the research of Bartolommeo Eustachio, 16th Century Italian author-physician. An accompanying text he wrote was lost, but the copper plates illustrating it were found and published in the 18th Century. The one above was considered the best illustration of the sympathetic nervous system done until recent times. Eustachio's name survives in the Eustachian tube to the ear, which he described.

nervous impulses that direct the stomach's reaction may both be unconscious, but the line between voluntary and involuntary begins to blur.

Not even a simple motor activity normally thought of as voluntary always stays in its conscious category. A person pushing a Ouija board pointer toward an "answer" that he hopes for may be entirely unconscious that he is pushing it at all.

Everything about human behavior suggests that man is a highly integrated creature, capable of coordinating and routing many nerve impulses to achieve a far greater range and choice of responses than any other animal. And there is no doubt that the organ that assesses the total situation and routes accordingly is the brain.

A switchboard, computer—and much besides

Since the 1900s, textbooks have compared the brain to a telephone switchboard; more recent books use the analogy of a computer. Both analogies do the brain an injustice. No switchboard or computer of man's invention can yet accomplish anything like the miracles of scrutinizing, sorting and remembering performed by the brain. But the analogies are functionally accurate. The brain is a switchboard—it connects incoming and outgoing calls. It is a computer—it makes decisions on which circuits to link. This is by no means a satisfying explanation of all our mental life, but it may be the bare beginning of an explanation. The vast computer-brain offers billions of circuits. Science has traced only a handful, and these with a clumsy forefinger in a microscopic world.

A simple look at the human brain suggests that it has specialized areas. Its bumps, hemispheres and tiny bodies have been grouped in a number of ways, but they can be seen as four geographic areas.

About 80 per cent of the brain is accounted for by what are known as the cerebral hemispheres, two large masses of nervous tissue which fill most of the skull. They are connected by a bridge of nerve fibers that enables them to work in association with each other. The surface of each cerebral hemisphere is thrown into a complex pattern of folds, known as convolutions, somewhat like those of a shelled walnut. This covering is called the cortex, and its convolutions evidently have much to do with intelligence. They are more complex in primates than in lower animals, and by far the most complex are found in man.

The cerebellum is also divided into two hemispheres. About the size of a pear, it is tucked underneath the rear projection of the cerebral hemispheres. Working below the level of consciousness, it helps to control equilibrium.

The limbic system, at the brain's center, consists of a number of small bodies, and seems to be a center affecting emotions. Recent experimental work suggests that, like the cortex, it plays a part in our conscious life.

CAPACITY FOR THINKING

The evolution of the brain, from prehistoric reptile to modern man *(below)*, has been linked to skull size. As the brain grew, allowing for more intricate thought processes, certain skull bones *(color)* expanded to accommodate it. Today man's cranial capacity averages about 80 cubic inches, roughly two thirds larger than a chimpanzee's. But the human brain has reached a plateau. It attained its present size in Neanderthal man 100,000 years ago.

EARLY REPTILE

PRIMATE

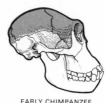

EARLY CHIMPANZEE

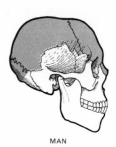

MAN

The thalamus and brainstem are beneath the cerebral hemispheres. The thalamus is a pair of egg-shaped bodies which act as integrating and routing stations for sensory nerves leading to the cortex. The brainstem is a body of tissue connecting the spinal cord and the rest of the brain. An upper section, the pons, is a bridge of connecting tissue between the two hemispheres of the cerebellum. A lower section, the medulla, helps control respiration, blood pressure and other vital autonomic functions. Both the thalamus and the brainstem work below the level of consciousness, but, like all the lower centers of the brain, have neural connections to the higher centers.

For centuries, certain portions of the brain have been held responsible for certain functions, but most early guesswork associated its parts with purely intellectual functions. Thus the idealistic Greeks believed that one part of the brain controlled fantasy, another part will, another part memory and so on.

"Moral taste" and "duty"

In the almost total absence of experimental research, speculation developed in the late 18th Century into the elaborate nonsense known as phrenology. It began with a Viennese physiologist, Franz Joseph Gall, who assumed that the bumps on a man's skull represented various areas of his brain that had been particularly well developed. His assumption was completely unfounded, for there is no relation between the brain's bumps and those of the skull bone. Nevertheless, Gall believed that a man's personality could be deduced by "reading" his skull bumps. He divided the brain into 37 areas, identifying each area with such traits as "moral taste," "self-esteem" and "duty." His ideas achieved enormous popularity. Europeans flocked to have their skulls read, and phrenological societies flourished in the wake of Gall's lecture tours.

But science was then becoming more sophisticated in its techniques and requirements of proof, and Gall's theories were regarded as quackery by most of his medical colleagues. A French physiologist, Pierre Flourens, attempted to disprove Gall by sound scientific methods: he removed portions of the brains of live pigeons to see what happened. His conclusion—that the brain operated as a single unit—was an over-simplification, but it helped refute Gall.

In 1861, a French surgeon, Pierre Paul Broca, performed an autopsy on the brain of an aphasic patient. Aphasics have perfectly normal vocal apparatus and apparently normal intelligence but cannot use words in speaking or writing. Broca opened up his patient's skull and found an area of visibly damaged cells, or lesion. This epochal discovery identified a particular area of the brain, now known as Broca's area, with the very distinctive function of verbal expression.

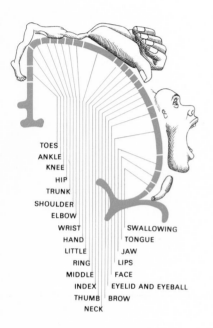

TOES
ANKLE
KNEE
HIP
TRUNK
SHOULDER
ELBOW
WRIST   SWALLOWING
HAND   TONGUE
LITTLE   JAW
RING   LIPS
MIDDLE   FACE
INDEX   EYELID AND EYEBALL
THUMB   BROW
NECK

DIVISION OF BRAIN POWER

This diagram of a misshapen man in odd-sized segments, was used by Dr.
Wilder Penfield to show the varying amounts of brain tissue controlling different parts of the body. The light brown line describes the shape of one hemisphere of the brain; it represents the strip of cortex that controls voluntary physical actions. Each segment indicates the location and size of the area controlling each part of the body, and the little man, called the "motor homunculus," shows graphically the proportionate amounts of brain tissue various parts receive. Hands, fingers and face have the most tissue devoted to them, trunk and shoulders the least.

The technique of removing parts of the brains of live animals, used by Flourens, was a fruitful one, and was followed by many later investigators. Gradually, specialized areas in the brain began to be charted.

By far the most interesting, as well as the most easily reached, area of the brain to work with was the cerebral hemispheres. Experimenters soon found that removing all or parts of them—a process known as decerebration—had far more radical effects on the behavior of higher animals than on lower.

After decerebration, a simple animal like a frog can see, jump and engage in sexual activity, although it loses its spontaneous liveliness. A cat loses many more functions. Depending on the area removed, it may become totally rigid and lose its sense of touch. It may recover its ability to walk, but seem reluctant to move. It may sit indefinitely until set in motion by the experimenter. In man, the loss of both cerebral hemispheres invariably results in death.

Such findings strongly suggested that the nervous structure of animals varies profoundly from species to species of animal. The nerve circuits controlling many functions in lower animals go only through the spinal cord or the lower brain centers, while in the organization of higher intelligence, the circuits controlling the same functions extend all the way to the cortex and back.

Attempts to map the human cortex with scientific accuracy were undertaken as soon as the electrical equipment was available. In 1870, two doctors in Berlin performed the first experiments in stimulating the cortex with electrodes, concentrating on dogs rather than humans. Since then, a great deal of exploration has been done with this technique. Using local anesthetics, Dr. Wilder Penfield, a brain surgeon with the Montreal Neurological Institute, has stimulated various parts of the cortex of epileptic patients to locate brain damage and has reported their oral descriptions of the effects.

The specialized brain

As a result of these and other experiments we now know positively that nervous impulses flowing through various areas of the cortex produce various effects, depending on the area. A strip of cortex in each hemisphere directs motor responses when stimulated, and damage in the same areas causes loss of motor function. Another area of the cortex is concerned with sensations of touch, others respectively with vision and hearing.

The brain, then, is an instrument with specialized parts. But its primary usefulness as a center for many kinds of circuits is its ability to choose, coordinate and integrate. Neurologists have seen sensory nerve cells in the retina of the eye. They have traced the optic nerve from the eye to the visual area of the cortex. They can even estimate the electrical resistance of a particular fiber from its diameter, so that they can compute how long it takes a nerve impulse to travel its length. They can stimulate the motor area of the cortex with an electrode, examine the nerve fiber endings in an eye muscle, and see the eye move. But what the human being perceives, and why he chooses to move his eyes one way rather than another way, are determined by events in the brain about which they know little or nothing.

It has fallen to psychologists rather than neurologists to show the integrating brain at work, knitting together various nerve processes into the single fabric of experience. They do not study neural impulses but attempt to analyze the web of consciousness by laboratory experiments on animals and human beings. One of their major fields of study has been our consciousness of the external world. They find it so elaborate that they hesitate to use such simple words as "see" and "hear." They prefer the word "perception" to describe a conscious impression of the external world. They use this term to indicate that something complicated has taken place—something far more complicated than the simple receipt of information from the sensory nerves.

For example, when we look at two men, one standing five feet away, the other 10 feet away, the visual image of the man farther away is only half the size of that of the nearer one. Yet we perceive at first glance that the two men are roughly the same height. To do so, we draw not only on sensory impressions but also on the whole body of our experience in a three-dimensional world. Experience has taught us how to interpret relative sizes according to distance. This feat seems ordinary—but only because the skill to perform it has been acquired with practice.

Every perception is a complicated weaving together of stimuli from the external world; of the immediate past (a lemon tastes sourer if it is taken immediately after a piece of sweet candy); of long experience, of interests and even of desires. In other words, perception involves physical, mental and emotional factors.

Many psychological experiments have given abundant proof of the fact that often we see what we expect to see. Here are a few:

• If the word "chack" is inserted in a sentence about poultry-raising, a proofreader is apt to misread it as "chick." If it appears in a sentence about banking, it will be misread as "check."

• One hundred military officers were shown two wooden blocks, one larger than the other, but both actually identical in weight. The officers were told the weight of the larger one, and asked to lift the smaller one and estimate its weight. They were evidently so surprised to find it heavier than its size led them to expect that they judged it to be even heavier than the large block. The illusion that it was heavier persisted even after the men had been permitted to weigh both blocks themselves.

• We also see what we want to see. Our emotional attitudes even affect the physiology of vision. It has been found that the pupils of the eyes dilate measurably upon looking at something we regard as pleasant. In one experiment, both men and women were shown a picture of a baby. The women's pupils dilated more than the men's. They dilated even wider at a picture of a mother and baby. The men's, on the other hand, dilated the most at a picture of a nude female.

• Subjects who were hungry saw more food objects in smudgy blurs than subjects who had just finished dinner.

• A group of rich children estimated the sizes of a series of coins as only slightly bigger than life-size. A group of poor children saw the coins as much as 50 per cent bigger. Quarters loomed particularly large.

Much of the work being done in psychological laboratories today raises large questions for the physiologist to answer tomorrow. Whether the mind is approached through the nerve tissue in the living body, or through its outward manifestations in behavior, it never appears simple. Neither the microscope nor the experimental laboratory has reduced it to a predictable machine. Among those who regard it with increasing respect are those scientists who know it best, and are keenly aware of how little they know.

The Intricate Art of Perception

When psychology was young, it was widely assumed that man's picture of the external world was a tapestry of sensations, and that the study of sensation would lead to much of man's mental life. Psychology today has come a long way from this simple proposition. It has found that man does not merely sense the world, he interprets it. As the psychologists say, he perceives. For example, different sensations may lead to the same interpretation. A man may read a book with his eyes, while a blind man reads the same book with his fingers. Both perceive the same meaningful words. Even a simple stimulus may be dramatically misinterpreted (*opposite*). Today, psychologists are still interested in man's grasp of the external world, but they are studying the many complicated ways in which he masters the aimless flow of sensation through acts of attention, interprets it according to his experience and needs, and perceives an intelligible world.

MISINTERPRETING SENSATIONS

A man in a dark room perceives a stationary light as making the movements he has drawn on the paper. Involuntary eye movements could make any light appear to move, but in most cases we know which lights are still, and perceive them accordingly. In this strange setting, the man has no glimpse of walls, no recognizable light source to guide him; hence he misinterprets his sensations.

ISOLATED HUMAN

Princeton graduate student Tom Wonnacott passes almost unendurable time in a sensory-deprivation experiment, unaware that he is being photographed by the light of infrared rays. His cell is pitch-black as well as soundproofed. Gloves blunt his sense of touch. The box at the foot of his bed is a refrigerator containing food. Wonnacott stayed in the cell for four days.

Released from his cell after four days, Wonnacott tried to hold a rod in a hole without hitting the sides. His agonizing effort failed.

Nothing to See or Hear

Man interprets sensations in order to perceive, but perception is nevertheless derived from sensations. It is man's continuous effort to understand his world. What happens when he is largely isolated from the sights, sounds and touch of the world?

This question has been under investigation since 1951, when pioneer work in sensory deprivation began at McGill University in Montreal. In more recent experiments at Princeton University, 55 volunteers were placed in solitary confinement in a dark, muffled room for periods of up to four days. They slept, thought and were bored. Some had hallucinations, which they found interesting rather than fearful. Tests during and immediately after confinement indicate that sensory deprivation alters perception in curious ways: time, instead of seeming longer, is telescoped; subjects become more sensitive to pain; hallucinations become more frequent as confinement is prolonged; shapes and figures are often distorted after confinement. If man is deprived of the normal flow of sensation, he can evidently muster his inner resources into a rational mental life for a while—but the strange experience seems to shake temporarily his ability to perceive normally.

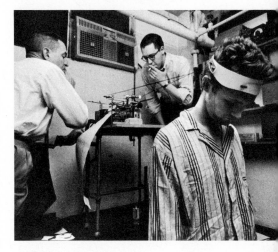

IMPAIRED ABILITIES

The picture above shows Wonnacott being subjected to a variety of tests minutes after his release. Most volunteers memorized word lists easily during confinement, but scored poorly in tests requiring comprehension afterwards. It took them about a day to get back to normal.

43

Exploring the Senses

Many of us go through life unaware of the subtlety and range of our senses, since we need only a fraction of their data to perceive the world well enough for our purposes. Yet we see and hear more than we think we do: a name we know fairly leaps from a page; a tape recording seems far fuller of background noises than real life, demonstrating that we are usually highly selective in what we listen to.

The handicapped show us how rich the senses really are. It is not true, for example, that the blind develop supernormal touch. All human beings have high concentrations of nerve endings in the fingertips, lips and tip of nose—sufficient to feel every dot of Braille. But the blind have an urgent motive for developing their perceptions of the fine messages these areas can send. Similarly, their skill in avoiding obstacles is due to their acute perception of echoes bouncing off objects as they approach—echoes every normal ear picks up, but that most people ignore as distractions.

Finally, recent work by psychologists in the United States under controlled conditions indicates that people may be able to distinguish colors with their fingertips and suggests that our sensory powers may be far greater than anyone previously dreamed.

SENSING COLOR

In an experiment at Queens College in Flushing, New York, a psychologist tests the responses of a subject to the feel of colored blocks. The reactions of the subject are recorded on an electroencephalograph machine shown in the background. Some scientists feel that man, like many lower organisms, may have light sensors scattered throughout his body.

READING WITH NOSE AND LIPS

In a home for war-wounded children in Rome during the '40s, Italo Renzetti, then aged 11 *(left)*, learned to read by pressing his nose and lips against the rough pages of a book in Braille. He was not only blind; both his arms had been amputated just below the shoulders as well.

44

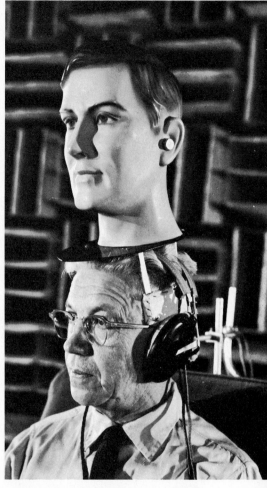

LISTENING FOR DISTANCE

Scientists have long believed that we gauge how far away a sound is by the different way it strikes each ear. The Bell Telephone physicist above is proving that we make unconscious turns of the head as we listen, favoring each ear in turn. He can hear sounds in the room only through microphones in the dummy's ears, connected to his earphones. As long as his own head moves the dummy, he can judge whether a sound is left or right. If he puts the dummy on a table, the sounds relayed from its two immobile ears give him little sense of direction.

GUIDED BY ECHOES

The time exposure at left shows a blind man with a light on his head skillfully zigzagging his way past screens as he hears echoes which warn him of obstacles. As the light reveals, the echoes are so slight he must sometimes come very close to an object to hear them.

A New Environment to Conquer

As man moves about the earth, he is constantly oriented by the pull of gravity. Up and down are always in place. Every motion is influenced, however unconsciously, by his familiarity with his own body weight.

In outer space, however, there is no gravity, no up, no down. Before man attempts to move about in it on long voyages, science must find out how well he can function when the most pervasive aspect of life on earth is absent. Tests like the one at left, and others that tumble astronauts about, indicate that neither cat nor man functions well when put in an unnatural position in relation to gravitational pull. But in a world without gravity, astronauts function very well.

UPSET CAT

A terrified cat *(above)* claws the air upon being suspended from the ceiling by means of magnets on its feet. Dr. Dietrich Beischer, warding off a possible fall, was testing the cat's adjustment to an upside-down world for possible application to astronauts. The cat paid no attention to the mice set to tempt it, and was removed from the ceiling after five frenzied minutes.

LEVEL-HEADED BIRD

A pigeon keeps its head imperturbably vertical while its body is moved about every which way. Gravity pulls on the fluid in the inner ear of most vertebrates and provides a keen sense of balance for the head. Thus both bird and man can perceive the world with steady gaze.

LIGHT LUNCH

In the padded cabin of a jet transport diving for 30 seconds at an acceleration that annihilates gravity, Frank Borman, Thomas Stafford (floating upside down) and James Lovell, all weight- less, have no trouble squeezing applesauce through straws. In tests like these, one third of the subjects said that weightlessness was mildly euphoric, as pleasant as floating in a tub.

More Than
Meets the Eye

There is more to human vision than the mechanics of the eye. Our eyes receive two-dimensional images on the screen of the retina, yet we perceive a three-dimensional world. The images from each eye offer valuable depth cues, such as relative sizes, objects overlapping other objects, and gradations of light, shadow and color. Further, since each of our eyes regards an object from a slightly different point of view, we receive two slightly different versions of the same scene. Normal vision is the fusing of these two images into a single picture with a three-dimensional look *(left)*.

This phenomenon is the principle behind the stereoscope, a visual device using a prism or mirror to endow flat pictures with an artificial third dimension. In the photographs on the opposite page, each right-hand scene is more than a simple reverse image of the left-hand scene; it is also shot from a slightly different position—as careful measurements will reveal. With the aid of a mirror, the right-hand scene can be reversed and made to merge with the left-hand scene. The diagram and caption below explain how this is done. The merger appears three-dimensional because of the small discrepancy between the pictures. The spiral staircase recedes high into the tower; the rifle and water ski jump out from the flat page.

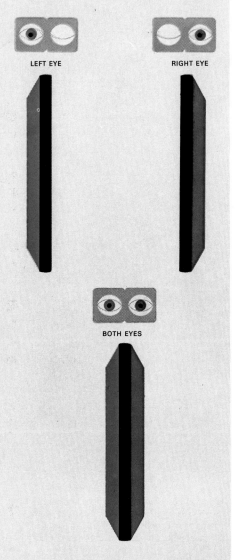

FUSING THE EYES' IMAGES
As the observer above looks at the book, each of his eyes receives a different image, as shown below. The left eye *(blue)* sees the spine and blue cover, the right eye *(red)* sees the spine and red cover. Although the brain receives a blurred "double exposure," it reconciles the discrepancy between the two fields of vision by perceiving one clear image of the book in depth.

LEFT EYE

RIGHT EYE

BOTH EYES

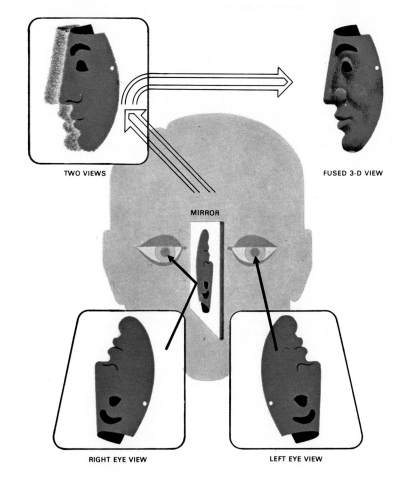

TWO VIEWS

FUSED 3-D VIEW

MIRROR

RIGHT EYE VIEW

LEFT EYE VIEW

ELEMENTARY STEREOSCOPE
The diagram above explains how the stereoscopic pictures on the opposite page can be fused with a mirror. The mirror is laid against the right side of the nose, with the eyes about six inches above a pair of pictures. The right eye looks at the reflection of the right-hand picture, the left eye looks at the left picture. The mirror is adjusted until the images coincide.

With the aid of a mirror, as shown on the opposite page, each pair of pictures above can be viewed as a three-dimensional scene.

The gargantuan boy in this unretouched photograph looms over the dog, his head apparently grazing the ceiling of a shuttered dollhouse.

The Case of the Rubber Boy

Sometimes, in his efforts to make sense of what he sees, man misinterprets reality. The two photographs above show a room especially constructed to create a false perception of distance.

The photographs are of the same room, same boy, same dog. The room, however, is a "distorted room" devised by the late Professor Adelbert Ames Jr. of Dartmouth College. It is made to be viewed with one eye through a peephole—although seeing it in a two-dimensional photograph

is equally deceptive. Either way eliminates binocular depth cues: the slight disparity between two images and the muscular swing of two eyes focusing together. Monocular cues are absent by design. On viewing the room, the observer assumes that walls, ceiling and floor meet at right angles, as in most rooms. Within this framework, obviously the boy and dog are the same distance away. They are beside windows that appear to be directly opposite; their feet are on floorboards that seem to be parallel.

But the Ames room is not a right-angled room. Ceiling and floor are trapezoids and, further, slope toward each other—the right wall is smaller than the left. The trapezoidal side windows are not opposite each other; the floorboards are not rectangular. The far left corner of the room is twice as far from the peephole as the right. Yet the viewer's misinterpretations are natural. A tall boy seems more reasonable than an absurdly shaped room. The illusion almost makes sense —until boy and dog change places.

Boy and dog have reversed positions and, apparently, relative sizes. They are really the same size: the mystery lies in the room itself.

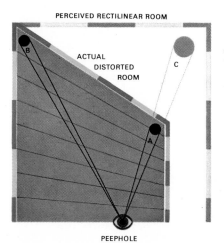

PERCEIVED RECTILINEAR ROOM

ACTUAL DISTORTED ROOM

PEEPHOLE

BLUEPRINT FOR DECEPTION
The light-brown area at left is the actual floor plan of an Ames room, the square is the room the observer supposes it to be. The boy at A appears to be much larger than the dog at B because the observer projects him to C. From this false perspective he appears unnaturally huge.

A FRAUDULENT ROOM EXPOSED
Boy and dog get together when one wall of the Ames room is removed, revealing the distorted construction *(right)*. The peephole used for the large photographs was located above the vertical post in forefront. This photograph was taken from a spot near the longer, left-hand wall.

Even when the viewer knows better, he sees the nest of circles *(left)* as a spiral, while the star shimmers and pulses uncontrollably.

Wrongheaded Sights

Man is determined to see things his own way. His way is sometimes imaginative, sometimes logical—and sometimes wrong.

For example, when many similar lines are crowded together, such as in the wheels at the bottom of the opposite page and the star at the right above, he perceives an illusory motion. The arrangement of the solid circles pictured above the wheels leads to a logical, if incorrect, interpretation: the one surrounded by big circles appears smaller than the one surrounded by little circles.

Perception is often confused by an unfamiliar background. The two pairs of parallels below are crossed by many background lines at many angles, but those at the center are close to right angles. Those at the ends are farthest from a right angle, so the white lines appear to bend there into a more perpendicular relationship. Finally, because of a spiraling pattern of squares in the background, the mind stubbornly sees the concentric circles above *(left)* as a spiral.

The pair of white lines at left appear to be converging, those at right to be slightly diverging. Actually both pairs are parallel.

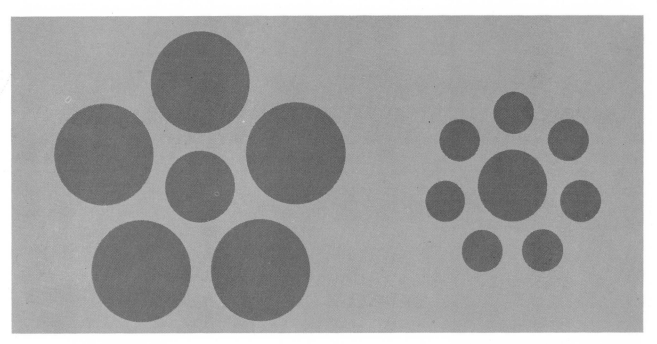

EQUALITY IN DISGUISE

In the two groups of circles above, the center circle at the left seems smaller than the center circle at the right. Both are actually the same size. The eye is deceived because of its ingrained habit of estimating sizes by the way they contrast with sizes of things around them.

NEW VIEWS

The phenomenon of reversible perspective is illustrated by the cubes above. The brown faces sometimes appear tops, sometimes bottoms. It is thought that, beneath the level of consciousness, perceptions alternate between stimulation and repose, and may shift to relieve fatigue.

WHEELS IN MOTION

The seven wheels surrounding the smaller gear *(right)* will all appear to spin clockwise if the book is held in two hands and moved in a fast, clockwise circle about two feet in diameter. At the same time, some observers also perceive the gear slowly rotating counterclockwise.

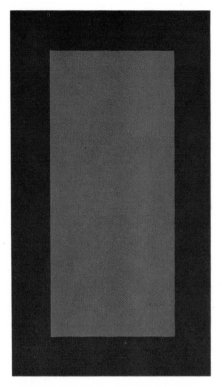
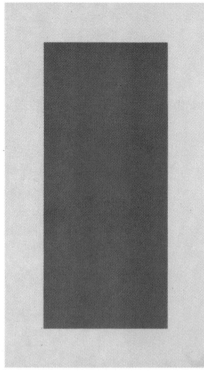

The Surprising Perception of Color

The human gift for interpreting sensory stimuli is nowhere more complicated than in its perception of colors. Physicists have long believed that color perceptions come from specific wavelengths of light, but recent revolutionary experiments indicate that colors can be perceived even in the absence of their specific wavelengths. We create colors from contrasts of shorter and longer wavelengths playing over an entire scene. Color is such a subjective experience that the effects produced on these two pages are properly called color "surprises" rather than illusions. All three effects depend on the fact that if the eye stares at one color, it begins to produce sensations of the complementary color—for reasons no one quite understands. Phenomena like this make modern psychologists concur with the 19th Century philosopher William James: "Whilst part of what we perceive comes through our senses from the object before us, another part (and it may be the larger part) always comes . . . out of our own head."

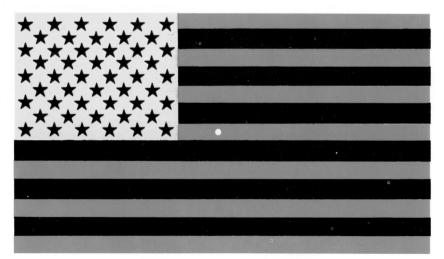

COMPLEMENTS OF "OLD GLORY"
Afterimages can come in complementary colors. If the eyes focus for 30 seconds on the small white dot in the center of the blue, black and yellow flag (left), then turn to look at any white area, a fleeting afterimage of the same flag in red, white and blue will be perceived.

A CONFUSION OF COLORS
As the eyes stare at the pattern opposite, the border between the red and turquoise shuttles back and forth, changes its contour, pulsates here, whirls there. The two colors are complementary, and the afterimages they arouse here give the strong impression of restless motion.

3

The Mind
under Stress and
in Disarray

FOR MANY CENTURIES the mentally ill were among the most tragic examples of man's inhumanity to man. Their behavior, sometimes bizarre, sometimes violent, caused their fellowmen to regard them with suspicion or distaste or outright hostility. At best, the mentally ill, or insane, were treated with callous indifference; at worst, with appalling cruelty. Cruelty toward the insane was particularly virulent in the 15th and 16th Centuries, when insanity was still thought to be a sign of possession by devils. Treatments were both ludicrous and fiendish, as shown in the picture essay which follows this chapter. And remnants of this kind of "therapy" persisted even when people no longer believed that lunacy meant possession by devils.

What are the causes of mental illness?

It is still uncertain whether or not they are organic, although it is known that organic problems can create disorders involving the mind. Sometimes nerve processes break down or perform abnormally because of injury to or degeneration of nerve tissues. The commonest of the degenerative diseases is cerebral arteriosclerosis, which hardens the arteries of the brain. Retardation and epilepsy can result from brain injury at birth. An accident to the brain may result in a loss of one or more motor functions. All these injuries and diseases are classified as organic because brain lesions or severed nerve fibers can be seen under the microscope. Doctors know what has gone wrong, though they may be unable to do anything about it. But people sometimes begin to behave in ways considered abnormal for no physical reason that can be detected. A broad range of mental illness stems from unknown causes.

Mental illness can affect behavior as drastically and conspicuously as an injured brain. It has wrought tragedy on a large scale from the beginnings of human history. In America today, some 600,000 mental patients are admitted to hospitals every year, and uncounted thousands more are being treated in clinics and by private physicians.

The medical specialty of psychiatry, devoted to the study and treatment of the mentally ill, no longer recognizes any clear-cut line between normal and abnormal. But a person may be said to be abnormal when his behavior seriously interferes with his work or with his ability to function in society. Most abnormal behavior is classified under two broad types: neurotic and psychotic. Neurotic behavior is close to the normal end of the spectrum; i.e., it is a milder form of abnormality. The neurotic patient may be abnormal only in certain areas of his life, and elsewhere perfectly rational. He often recognizes his trouble and may be able to contribute to his recovery. A psychosis is far more serious, and it makes itself manifest in all aspects of the psychotic's behavior. A psychotic is a person who has lost some or all contact with reality.

The causes of neuroses are now widely assumed to be environmental;

WITHOUT HOPE
This picture of a forlorn patient in a dismal mental hospital was taken for LIFE in 1946 by photographer Jerry Cooke, and became part of the famous "Family of Man" photographic collection. As a document, it dramatically focused public attention on the lot of many of the eight million mentally ill of the time: years in neglected institutions, with only nominal therapy.

i.e., caused by the stresses and strains of life. All adults—and many children—encounter stresses, and it is a rare adult who does not use what psychiatrists call neurotic defenses to cope with them. There are people who are habitually late, some who are obsessed with tidiness and some who are maddeningly forgetful of appointments. Neurotics use ruses to call attention to themselves or to win praise or to erase unpleasant thoughts from their minds. As a rule, they do these things because they are timid, or suspect they are really untidy and therefore undeserving, or wish to avoid something with unpleasant connotations for them. The root of all neuroses, in other words, is emotional conflict.

Below consciousness and above

Neuroses show themselves in many different symptoms. Here are a few of them:

ANXIETY STATE: Every emotional conflict causes a certain amount of anxiety. If the conflict is severe, so is the anxiety. If there is no easy solution for a serious emotional conflict, the victim may have to live with it as best he can. At times the conflict may be shoved below consciousness, and at times it may pop up, but it always causes considerable anxiety. For example, a grown son may be constantly irritated by a senile parent who lives in the house with him, but he can neither dispose of the parent nor express his irritation without feeling guilty. Over the years the son pretends that all is well between him and his parent. But he cannot hide the associated anxiety. His anxiety, in psychiatric terminology, becomes "free-floating" because to him it has no apparent cause. The fact that it has no apparent cause adds still further to the victim's distress. He may be constantly worried and tense, lose his appetite and suffer from insomnia and general fatigue. His heart may unaccountably beat too fast, or he may have fits of trembling or difficulty in breathing. In a number of ways, an anxiety state can create acute stages of physical impairment.

HYPOCHONDRIA: Where the anxious neurotic gives expression to his anxiety and tries to live with his problems, the hypochondriac attempts escape as his solution. An employee who fears his boss may, upon seeing him approach, suffer the symptoms of an anxiety state. He complains of illness. If once he succeeds in avoiding an unpleasant encounter by way of the infirmary, he may thereafter find himself ill every time he anticipates another unwelcome meeting.

The imaginary illnesses of hypochondriacs do not usually fit the descriptions of any known disease, but hypochondriacs are usually adept at providing their own "diagnoses." A hypochondriac generally puts forth the most gloomy predictions on his condition, but he is not truly anxious about it—not as anxious, certainly, as he would be if the illness were real. Like most neurotic escapes, hypochondria creates more prob-

THE DANCE OF LUNACY

Under a leering moon five women, crazed by moonlight, dance dementedly in this illustration of lunacy—literally moon-madness. Nearly every culture has believed such external forces as the "evil" moon arbitrarily caused madness. The word "lunatic"—one who is moonstruck—derives from the Latin *Luna,* the moon goddess. Such explanations for insanity were common even in sophisticated Europe until the 18th Century.

lems for the sufferer than it solves. In the end, not only his ability to work but also his pleasure in life may be seriously impaired.

HYSTERIA: Sometimes a neurotic will escape from his conflict through the process of coming down with physical symptoms of a real disease. Hysteria is the name given to this category of mental illness. (It is not to be confused with the popular conception of hysterics as bouts of weeping or screaming by women in fits of temper or fear.) Under hysteria, a soldier in mortal fear of being sent into combat may suddenly be unable to see. Although there is nothing organically wrong with his eyes, he is quite literally blind. Hysteria can produce such exact symptoms of genuine illness that hysterical maladies have been operated on as a result of incorrect diagnoses by misled surgeons.

PHOBIA: "Phobia" means fear, and a neurotic phobia is an irrational fear of something that substitutes for a true, but hidden, fear. For example, a married woman is attracted to her neighborhood grocer. Fearful of the consequences of this attraction, she pretends that it does not exist. Walking home from the grocery store, she finds herself frightened by the traffic whizzing by. She ascribes her fright to a fear of being run over. From then on, she never goes to the grocery store because of her newly developed phobia about "traffic"—not merely on the way to the store but everywhere. She avoids the grocer by sending her husband or a child to do the shopping, but since traffic is an inescapable condition of modern life, she is a prisoner caged at home by her phobia.

DEPRESSION: Neurotic depression is a prolonged case of grief and low spirits. It may follow a severe illness or bereavement, during which the sufferer is persistently plagued by feelings of discouragement, failure and inferiority. He puts a gloomy interpretation even on things that are going well for him. Neurotic depression represents not an escape from fear but a surrender to it.

In general, no matter what forms his symptoms take, the neurotic not only finds life difficult, but is difficult for others to live with. His quirks and the limitations on his activities rouse irritation in normal people.

The psychotic's world

The psychotic presents an altogether different picture. Where the neurotic is difficult and incapacitated only in some respects, the psychotic represents human wastage and suffering on a large scale. Psychoses do have mild phases, and sometimes mild psychotics can be treated on an outpatient basis, but usually they must be hospitalized. Their symptoms tell of a world completely apart from the one normal persons know: it is a world of delusions, hallucinations, garbled speech, garbled thoughts and exaggerated emotional states.

Most of the patients in mental hospitals are sent there for treatment

THE FACE OF MADNESS
His face distorted by rage, a captive madman suffers in a 19th Century British insane asylum. The drawing is by Sir Charles Bell, the British surgeon, who illustrated his own book, *The Anatomy of Expression*. By this time, physicians were beginning to look for physiological explanations for madness. They no longer believed it was caused by an external visitation which could be cured by torture or exorcism.

of two main types of psychosis: schizophrenia and manic-depression.

SCHIZOPHRENIA: The term means "fragmenting of personality." A schizophrenic is unable to concentrate on one idea or one train of thought. His speech and behavior are confused and disconnected, full of phrases and acts that may mean something to him but make no sense to an observer. A schizophrenic patient may suddenly shout, "Don't poison me!" when no food or drink is offered him. He may spend all day sweeping the room with an imaginary broom.

Schizophrenia is by far the more common of the two main types of psychosis, and many variations of schizophrenia are distinguished by psychiatrists. The four principal ones are known as simple schizophrenia, hebephrenia, catatonia and paranoia.

"Apathetic, listless, dull-witted"

SIMPLE SCHIZOPHRENIA: The simple schizophrenic lives in an emotionally insulated state. He is aware of the outside world, but indifferent to it, withdrawn from it. He is apathetic, listless, dull-witted. Other people mean little to him. Simple schizophrenics are sometimes not recognized as such by those around them, and psychiatrists believe that many of them drift untreated along the fringes of society, as tramps, prostitutes and petty criminals. As a rule, they are incapable of productive work other than the most menial kinds.

HEBEPHRENIA: The hebephrenic retrogresses into infantile behavior. He talks baby talk, becomes incoherent, lapses into silliness and sudden, pointless laughter. He gesticulates and grimaces extravagantly; he becomes careless and sometimes gross in personal hygiene.

CATATONIA: The catatonic alternates between complete physical immobility and demonic frenzy. He will sit immobilized for hours, even days, then may abruptly become wildly excited, attacking anyone near him or tearing at himself with his fingernails. In his immobile state he is very suggestible: he may rouse himself to repeat phrases, take orders or imitate a gesture.

PARANOIA: The paranoid schizophrenic presents the classic symptoms of madness. His utterly illogical behavior actually has a reason behind it, for he suffers from delusions of grandeur, of persecution or of eroticism. He hears voices that are not spoken and sees people who are not there. His delusion may grow until he imagines himself the center of a worldwide conspiracy, involving, say, the entire apparatus of the U.S. Government, or the Catholic Church, or the Communist Party. Every passing stranger is a spy, and those closest to him too are implicated in the plot. In fact, spies surround him. He may believe that radar waves are being directed at his brain to control his thoughts. He may attribute his worldwide importance to the fact that he is Napoleon or Jesus Christ.

AN ATTACK OF BELONEPHOBIA

A phobia, or fear, of sharp objects (*belone* is Greek for "needle") has made the man in this cartoon faint. Everyone has fears, but fears are considered phobias only when they are so unreasonable that they interfere with normal life. Below are listed a few of the more than 250 things doctors have found patients to be abnormally afraid of, with the medical names for the phobias.

Books	Bibliophobia
Cats	Ailurophobia
Confined spaces	Claustrophobia
Heights	Acrophobia
Night	Noctiphobia
Ridicule	Categelophobia
Being stared at	Ophthalmophobia
Strange people	Xenophobia
String	Linonophobia
13	Triskaidekaphobia
Work	Ergophobia
Fear	Phobophobia

Paranoids may swing from withdrawal to violence, during which a total stranger may be attacked with homicidal vigor.

MANIC-DEPRESSION: Much less prevalent than schizophrenia, manic-depression does not always involve delusions or hallucinations. Here it is the victim's emotions that are beyond control. Attacks of manic-depression are usually rhythmic. The victim may have periods of normalcy between bouts, although one attack may last for months. His attacks may alternate between the two phases of the ailment, rendering him manic for a period, and then putting him into a state of depression.

MANIA: The term means a state of excitement or elation. The mildly manic patient seems flighty, overactive, overconfident. He is brilliant, aggressive and sociable, but domineering and intolerant of criticism. As the illness progresses he becomes unable to keep still vocally or physically; he sings and talks incessantly, paces back and forth, bangs himself against walls. In the most serious stages he becomes delirious.

DEPRESSION: Psychotic depression begins with feelings of dejection and discouragement. The victim sits alone, contemplating his sins. As the depression deepens, he holds himself responsible for all sorts of catastrophes—floods, plagues, earthquakes. Severely disturbed depressives may retreat to complete inaction. Then they become totally bedridden, refusing to function in any way at all.

What's right, what's wrong?

In addition to the neuroses and psychoses, there are mental illnesses grouped under the rubric of character disorders. The main victims are psychopaths, who appear outwardly intelligent and normal, but seem to be incapable of emotional depth. They have few, if any, feelings of right and wrong, and are totally unconcerned about the consequences of their acts. Tests show that psychopaths actually feel less anxiety about threats of physical pain than normal persons. Their unconcerned readiness to cheat, steal and even murder naturally makes them grave threats to society.

The causes of the mental illnesses described above constitute the most important unsettled question of modern psychiatry. Answers have been given, but none of them are conclusive. This is the basic question, still largely unsolved: where and how does abnormality originate?

Some experts in pathology believe that the origins can be found in early environmental causes—in the elaborate and often precarious formation of personality in childhood. Others believe that the origins are in the genes—in a faulty physiological heritage. Each group can marshal persuasive evidence.

The environmentalists are supported by a study conducted in Chicago in the late 1930s by two sociologists, R.E.L. Faris and H. W. Dunham.

UNBEARABLE SHAME

Shamed by Hamlet's dismissal of her love, stricken by the death of Polonius, her father, an insane Ophelia leans forward to hang flowers on a bough. The branch she holds for support soon snaps and the girl, "incapable of her own distress," drowns. Ophelia's withdrawal from reality and her senseless verbal ramblings are marks of schizophrenia. In an age when insanity was little understood, Shakespeare described madness with what one expert terms "almost clinical accuracy."

In the course of investigating the effects of urban living upon personality, the two men found a much greater incidence of schizophrenia in slums than in better-class neighborhoods. They suggested that schizophrenia was a poor-man's disease and argued that the stresses of poverty contributed to its incidence. But biologically oriented scientists dispute the conclusion. They say that the higher incidence of schizophrenia in slums merely proves that people incapacitated by a poor genetic endowment tend to sink in the social scale.

The case for the genetic theory

One of the most interesting pieces of evidence in support of the biological theory is a study conducted in the 1940s by psychiatrist Franz Kallmann of New York. His project traced the recurrence of schizophrenia within families. Kallmann reasoned that if the disease was genetic in origin, it ought to occur with equal frequency among identical twins. He studied the case histories of identical twins, whose genes were of course identical. He found that when one identical twin became schizophrenic the chances were almost nine out of 10 that the other twin followed suit. In the case of fraternal twins, whose genes are similar but not identical, the chances of both becoming schizophrenic were less than two in 10.

In the absence of more certain knowledge, most psychiatrists proceed on the supposition that both environment and heredity are factors in psychosis. Genetic flaws capable of affecting the nervous system may be present, but produce serious disturbances only under conditions of environmental stress.

Fortunately, treatment of psychotics has not had to wait for hypotheses to be proved. Treatment has moved ahead rapidly in the last 50 years, often on the basis of theory, more often on the practical basis of what works. It has resulted in increasing numbers of treatments.

For many years the most widely used treatment for hospitalized psychotics was shock. The earliest shock treatments used insulin injected into the muscles to produce a state of coma. This method has largely been replaced by electroshock, in which an electric current is passed through the frontal area of the brain producing convulsions. Shock does not cure a patient. It simply relieves his symptoms temporarily, bringing him back to reality so that he can be receptive to various forms of psychotherapy.

In recent years shock therapy has been almost entirely replaced by the use of the new tranquilizer and antidepressant drugs. These calm hyperactive patients and lift stuporous ones out of their lethargy. Like shock treatment, they do not cure in themselves, but they prepare the patient for longer-range psychotherapy. A great range of several hundred

VIOLENT CURES

Lampooning the medical profession, a 17th Century German cartoon shows a fictional Doctor Würmbrandt and an aide "curing" mental disease. Doctors of the time treated mental illness with a trinity of drastic physical measures, emetics, purgatives and bloodletting, with little effect on madness. In this case, the satirist shows a purgative being administered *(left)* and a madman's head being thrust into a kiln to drive out demons.

drugs has been developed in recent years, revolutionizing the treatment of the mentally ill.

For some time past, psychopathologists have questioned the adverse effect of the hospital itself upon the mental patients. Most hospitals, especially state mental hospitals, are large, overcrowded and understaffed. It is practically impossible to give each patient close personal attention. Left to itself in this environment, an unstable personality grows worse. Some schizophrenics and depressives are now being treated experimentally on an outpatient basis when the relative mildness of the disorder, plus the controlling effect of drugs, makes this arrangement practical. The patient goes to work each day and returns to the hospital at night, or he comes to the hospital for treatment during the day and returns to his home at night.

The lady of the towels

Still another new and practical treatment recently tried on psychotic patients runs counter to the orthodoxy of psychotherapists, including Freudian analysts, who believe that the causes of the disorder must be discovered and recognized before the *symptoms* can be removed. The new procedure is an outgrowth of behaviorist psychology which for years has been experimenting with animals on altering behavior patterns. Behavior therapy attempts to alter psychotic behavior without trying first to determine the underlying causes. And sometimes behavior therapists have achieved remarkable results. Consider, for example, the case history reported by psychologist Teodoro Ayllon of a patient at the Saskatchewan Hospital in Canada.

His patient was a woman of 47, a chronic schizophrenic who had been hospitalized for nine years. She weighed more than 250 pounds; she hoarded towels; she dressed in layer upon layer of clothes, with as many as 18 pairs of stockings, several dresses, sweaters, plus towels and sheets draped around her or over her head; she always carried around three cups, a bundle of miscellaneous clothing and an outsized purse.

The patient had attained her gross weight by eating food she stole from other patients in the dining room or from the counter. Under Dr. Ayllon's regime she was given a table to herself and presented with the special diet prescribed for her. The minute she moved from her table to go to others or to the food counter, she was taken out of the room, thereby missing part or all of her meal. Within two weeks she gave up trying to supplement her diet through theft, and her weight began to drop. Eventually her weight dropped to 180 pounds.

The towel problem was tackled in reverse fashion. Instead of trying to keep her from getting extra towels from the storeroom or from other patients' rooms, she was given extra towels, at first seven towels daily

BRAIN SURGERY

Centuries of search for physical cures of mental disease led by the 1930s to the use of brain surgery for violent cases. In the prefrontal lobotomy, fibers between the thalamus and the cortex are cut. The topectomy is the removal of parts of the cortex. In the thalamotomy, an electric needle destroys some of the thalamus itself. Today, drugs have largely replaced brain surgery, which is now used most often in cases of unbearable pain.

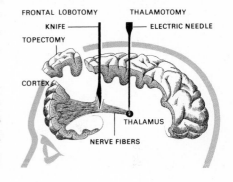

and gradually up to 60 towels daily. Eventually she had 625 towels in her room, folded and piled up practically on every available inch of space. Then she began to resist. She threw towels out of the room and refused to accept any when the nurses continued to bring them to her. When the extra-towel supply was discontinued, she was content with the regular quota.

The clothing problem was met by placing a scale near the dining-room entrance after her weight was satisfactory. Having calculated that she habitually wore perhaps 20 or so pounds of extra clothes, a system was established to weigh her before letting her enter to take her meal. A quota for loss of additional weight was established for each meal. If she did not make the quota she would have to forgo her meal. She began to shed. The cups and the bundle went. Then she began taking off outer layers of dresses and sweaters and stockings. Eventually she was dressing normally. Her family came to see her at this stage, and for the first time in nine years wanted to take her home with them for a visit.

Orthodox psychotherapy would argue that the symptoms that were eliminated would either reappear or be replaced by other forms of behavior equally abnormal. In the case of this patient, only one symptom reappeared: twice over a span of a year she reverted to attempts to steal food. No other unwelcome symptoms appeared.

Mental Illness, from Demonology to Therapy

For centuries, society has made the mentally ill pay a heavy price for their affliction. Their bizarre behavior has long aroused the cruel hostility of ignorance. In early Christian times, madmen were believed to be inhabited by devils and were literally cast forth to live as they might, although monasteries sheltered some. By the 15th Century, neglect turned to active persecution: the mentally ill were tortured and burned alive. Although with the Renaissance men began to ascribe madness to physical causes, it still seemed a just punishment—probably for a wicked life. The insane were imprisoned, chained to the floor. Only with the turn of this century have new medical knowledge and the discovery of the unconscious provided keys to understanding. The sympathetic treatment offered by many public hospitals today, supported by society itself, is a belated recognition of the fact that the forces bedeviling the mentally ill bedevil us all.

THE MAD TREATING THE MAD
A quack surgeon plucks "the stone of folly" from a fool's head while a monk assists and a nun looks on vacantly in this 16th Century painting by Hieronymus Bosch *(pages 136, 137)*. The surgeon's funnel is symbolic of fraud, his jug a symbol of Satan. Bosch was satirizing the ignorance of his day, when surgeons commonly deluded patients into believing such stones caused madness.

Exorcism by Faith and Flame

The belief that the mentally ill were seized by demons was handed on to the Middle Ages from the Greeks and Romans, but the ancients treated their mentally ill with religious ceremonies and kindness. With the fall of the Roman Empire and the collapse of social institutions, the insane were often literally uncared for. Madmen often were forced to hide in the woods. Monasteries were the only asylums for the insane, and prayers the principal therapy. And in that era of strong belief, exorcism and faith healing were often effective (*right*).

But by the 15th Century, a beleaguered faith had become defensive. Wars, chaos and the Black Death gave rise to epidemics of madness—mass dancing, mass delusions—which in turn led to mass witch hunts. The Inquisition held that any madman or madwoman was a dangerous wizard or witch. If torture failed to expel the devil, fire was used. In Trèves 7,000 witches were burned over a period of several years; in Geneva over 500 were burned in the year 1515 alone. As one 16th Century historian wrote, "All over Germany pyres are blazing; the flames of execution are red."

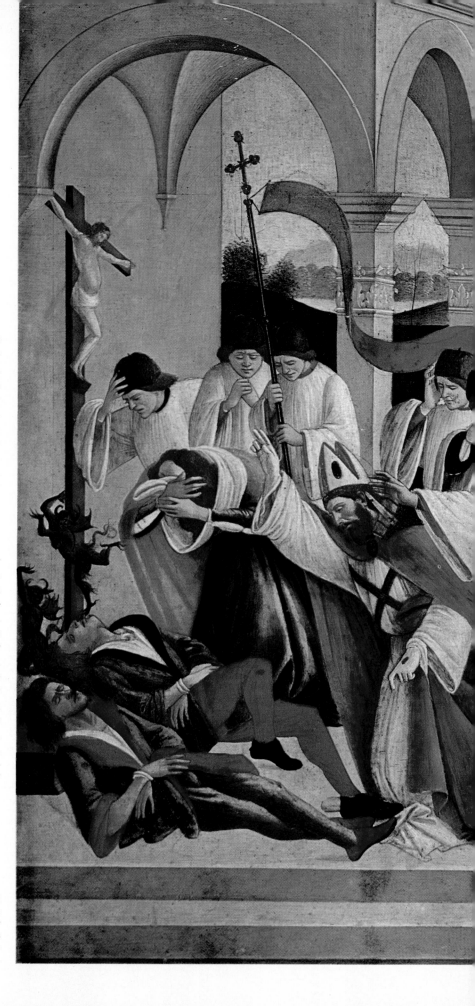

THE POWER OF EXORCISM
Devils flee from the mouths of the possessed as St. Zenobius exorcises them in this 16th Century painting. Zenobius, a Fourth Century bishop, performed a number of such miracles of healing. At that time exorcism was a gentle ceremony, a simple invocation of God's power.

THE POWER OF SAINTS

The 13th Century shrine of St. Dympna located in Gheel, Belgium, whose altar is seen above, was built after five lunatics were miraculously cured on the spot. Attracting pilgrimages of the mentally ill from all over Europe, Gheel became the center of a colony for the insane. According to legend, St. Dympna was beheaded here by her father while the devil looked happily on.

THE POWER OF FIRE

Three witches burn and a demon which has plagued one of them departs, issuing backward from her mouth. The devil in this 1555 woodcut appears as a monster with breasts of the human female. Other drawings of the period show him as a toad, a spider, as blood or as fumes. The text from Exodus, "Thou shalt not suffer a witch to live," was used to justify death by fire.

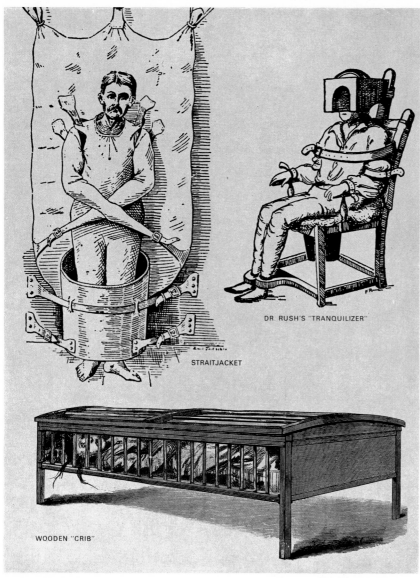

STRAITJACKET

DR. RUSH'S "TRANQUILIZER"

WOODEN "CRIB"

The devices at left were used throughout the 19th Century to constrain violent cases. But Dr. Benjamin Rush, often called "the father of American psychiatry," thought of his "tranquilizer" as more than a constraint, being convinced that total inaction was therapeutic.

The Expedient of Confinement

In the Renaissance, secular authority replaced Church power in many areas of life. Monasteries relinquished the care of mental patients to society at large, which simply imprisoned them. In 1547, the London monastery of St. Mary of Bethlehem became the city hospital commonly called "Bedlam" (right). There, as in most asylums, patients were chained among criminals. Society's conscience was unbothered—indeed it came to stare. The setting encouraged sadism. Wardens beat the violent; others were bled, blistered and purged in the name of therapy. By the 19th Century, some physicians, although baffled by the disease they sought to cure, at least fought to improve living conditions. Dr. Benjamin Rush, who instituted the first course in psychiatry in America about 1800, provided patients with warm rooms and decent attendants. But even he was misled by the ignorance of an era when, as one doctor later observed, "by bleeding them to faintness it was believed [the insane] were cured."

THE STRIPPING OF DIGNITY

Cooling His Brains, an 18th Century cartoon, depicts the British statesman Edmund Burke as a madman. Beyond its contemporary political import, the picture shows how patients were treated on admission: their hair shaved, one leg and one arm fettered to the floor with chains.

THE PRICE OF SIN

The last of William Hogarth's moralistic series of paintings, *A Rake's Progress,* brings the rake to Bedlam, now mad after his life of sin. His mistress grieves, while visiting ladies stand by, amused. The 18th Century painter used Bedlam as the very pit of human degeneration.

"To Free These Beasts"

In 1793, in a Paris seething with revolutionary ideas, Philippe Pinel was appointed physician to Bicêtre, a hellhole into which the city thrust its madmen. Pinel had revolutionary ideas of his own, one of which was to free patients from their chains. When he told the prison commissioner of his plans, the commissioner asked, "Are you not yourself mad to free these beasts?" Pinel replied, "I am convinced that the *people* are not incurable if they can have air and liberty." And Pinel gave his patients fresh air and freedom. The first "beast" to be unfettered had lived in chains and darkness for 40 years. When he saw the sky, he cried, "How beautiful!" The second, 10 years in chains, recovered and became Pinel's bodyguard.

Finding his policies fully justified at Bicêtre, Pinel went on to reform Salpêtrière *(left)*, the Paris hospital for demented women. He provided exercise, concerts, reading and visits with friends. The most noted of the reformers, Pinel was not altogether alone. During the same period, Vincenzio Chiarugi in Italy was releasing the insane from chains, and in England the Quaker York Retreat practiced kindness toward the mentally ill.

PIONEER OF KINDNESS
Philippe Pinel supervises the unshackling of mental patients in a Paris asylum for women in 1796. The physician's bold reforms were regarded as dangerous, even mad. Few were prepared to accept his observation that "kindness has the most favorable effect on the insane."

NEW PATTERNS
A patient at Manhattan State Hospital in New York City, encouraged by a nurse, weaves a rug in an occupational therapy room. Arteriosclerosis has damaged a portion of her brain, but the skill and concentration required in weaving help renew her dexterity and self-confidence.

ARTISTIC SELF-EXPRESSION
Two women *(left)* paint in the art therapy program. Through this visual medium patients sometimes reveal anxieties they are unable to put into words. The staff gains insight, and patients sometimes come to see their problems clearly for the first time—an invaluable therapy.

STEPPING OUT TOWARD OTHERS
Dancing a reel to the rhythm of an improvised percussion band, patients acquire a new ease and confidence in their relations with others. Often fearful of other people at first, the patients learn to relax here as a volunteer worker *(far right)* coaches them in their performance.

No Cheap and Easy Cure

The pictures on these pages, taken at Manhattan State Hospital in New York City, show the improvement in the care of the mentally ill that has been achieved in the last 150 years, thanks to prodding by reformers like Philippe Pinel. Fifty years after Pinel had unchained his patients in France, Dorothea Dix in the U.S. was pleading with Congress to act on behalf of the "insane . . . bound with galling chains, bowed beneath fetters, lacerated with ropes." Her crusade was begun in the 1840s, and over the next 50 years treatment of the insane was gradually transferred from local communities to the states. The growth of the state hospital system firmly established in America the principle of humane professional care for all the mentally ill.

It has proved a difficult and expensive policy to live up to, however. In this century, state institutions became crowded with long-term patients. The depression of the 1930s reduced many institutional budgets to bare subsistence levels, and World War II depleted trained staffs. This period has been called the "dark age" for American mental patients.

In the 1950s the use of new drugs and other therapies helped change public mental hospitals from largely custodial institutions to places of real hope. Their average budget is still less than six dollars per patient per day, compared to $45 for psychiatric care in private hospitals. Their staffs are still underpaid and overworked. Yet they are now returning thousands of their patients annually to society. What they might do with more public support is an enticing thought.

WELL-DIRECTED VIOLENCE
A hard right at a punching bag in Manhattan State's gymnasium helps focus this slugger's hostility without injury to himself or to others.

ARRIVAL IN THE WARD

Ann Clark, just arrived at Manhattan State Hospital, has been helped into pajamas and a robe by nurses. Inwardly she is far more agitated than she looks. Shortly before, she had been weeping at being brought here; now she has withdrawn, convinced that everyone around her is hostile. Her behavior at home had been so strange that a neighbor called the police.

First Day: Out of Reach

These pages begin the story of the treatment one woman recently received at Manhattan State Hospital. On a winter's day in 1964, Mrs. Ann Clark (a fictitious name but a real person) was brought to the hospital with symptoms that indicated schizophrenia: withdrawal into fantasy and delusions of persecution.

Ann had spent some of her childhood in a foster home. She had left high school after two years, worked in a factory, married in her early twenties. After separating from her husband she had a son, whom she put in a foster home. Shy and seclusive, she nevertheless quarreled often with her mother and friends. She was first hospitalized in her twenties, after threatening suicide. Two years later she was hospitalized again, believing people were trying to kill her.

Ann was discharged after two years, remarried, and her new husband had accepted her son into the household. But again delusions threatened her. These pictures were taken by LIFE photographer Alfred Eisenstaedt with the permission of Dr. Oscar K. Diamond, Manhattan State's director.

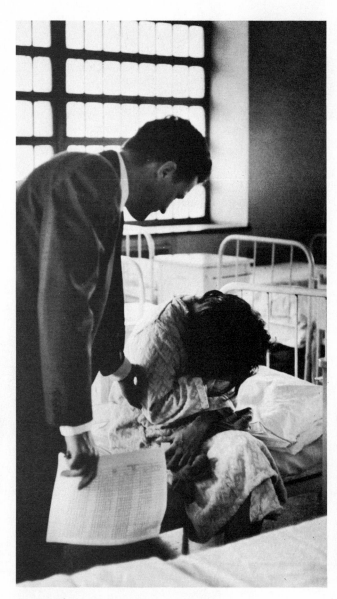 

PRELIMINARY INTERVIEW
Ann burst out crying again when Dr. Dusan Mavrovic, Director of Female Admissions, introduced himself and tried to speak to her. Repeatedly assuring her that he wanted to help, Dr. Mavrovic led her to an office. There she gave short, almost inaudible replies to his questions. "Do you feel depressed now?" "Slightly." "Why are you crying so much?" "I miss my child." "How is your child?" She smiled briefly. "He's in very good health." But soon she hid her face with her hand and only shrugged her shoulders to the doctor's further questions.

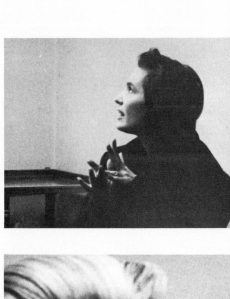

Ann drinks her first dose of chlorpromazine—a tranquilizer she took four times daily.

Second Stage: Opening Up

New drugs, such as the chlorpromazine Ann was given, are not complete cures, but they may relieve psychotic symptoms, so that patients can begin to talk about their problems. By her third day at Manhattan State, Ann was able to respond to Dr. Daniel D. Sparks, the psychiatrist assigned to her, and describe the state of mind that led to her commitment.

Like many mental patients, Ann ascribed her relapse into the uncontrollable anxieties of mental illness to physical causes. She told Dr. Sparks she had been eating and sleeping poorly, had become "run down." Soon she was too "nervous" to do household chores. Her anxieties created a vicious circle—the more they grew the more frightened she was to seek help. One day she and her husband and son took a walk in the park. Ann was suddenly terrified by all the people around her. It was an unspeakable terror. She told her husband she wanted to buy some ice cream, left him and the boy and ran home. When she reached their apartment, she locked herself in. It was fears of this magnitude, which no locked door could shut out, that the hospital would now try to help her manage. Her self-confidence was bolstered by an intensive program of specially prescribed therapies. In regular sessions Dr. Sparks encouraged her to talk about the fears, discussed realistic ways of coping with them. Together, these treatments helped restore Ann's mastery over her emotions.

EXPRESSIONS OF CONFIDENCE

By the third day, Ann presents a different picture. She is dressed in daytime clothes and calmed by doses of chlorpromazine. In the pictures at left and below she is able to tell her psychiatrist, Dr. Sparks, with animated gestures, of events that led to her hospitalization. At this stage she is still fearful of strangers, and her trust in Dr. Sparks is an important step forward.

Discharge:
A World to Face

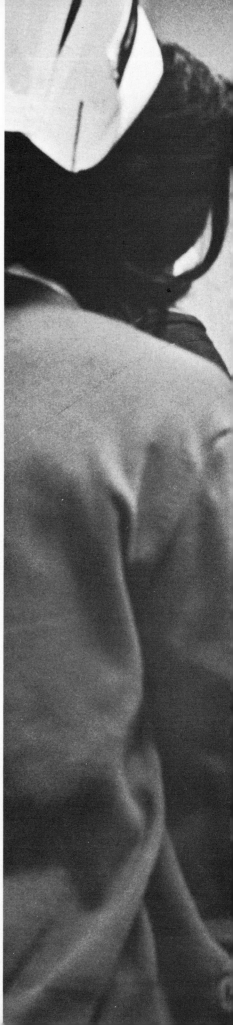

Ann's progress was rapid, and by the sixth week of her stay at Manhattan State, Dr. Sparks felt she was emotionally strong enough to leave the sheltering hospital and go home. A social worker visited Ann's husband and found him a patient, hard-working man, eager to greet his wife and cooperate with the hospital's recommendations for her aftercare. In April, Ann was released on convalescent status. Her mental health would now depend on visits to a community clinic for periodic treatments, on medication which she would continue to take, and on the understanding she found in her family and community. The possibility of "complete cure" is one which the hospital's director, Dr. Diamond, compares to curing a patient of pneumonia. "The person who sits in a draft and comes down with pneumonia can of course be hospitalized and cured. But if he returns to the same draft, he'll come down with the same disease. For the mentally ill, that draft is the total lack of understanding in the society they live in." Until society changes, treatment of the mentally ill must consist of the difficult job of strengthening them to live with misunderstanding.

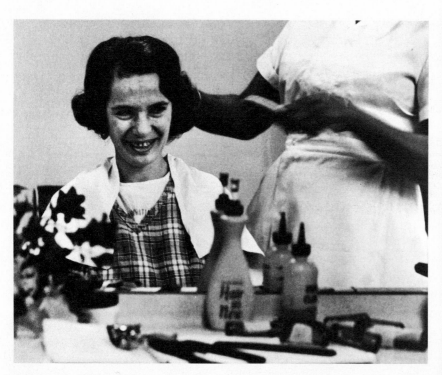

PRETTY TO LOOK AT
By her third week, Ann cared enough about appearances to benefit from a visit to the hospital's beauty shop. Interest in a new hairdo is an important sign of recovery. To Ann, every glance had once been hostile. Now she could not only bear them, she was brave enough to invite them.

"IT'S BEEN AWFULLY NICE"
Dismissed after almost seven weeks in the hospital, Ann pauses to sign out for her only belonging checked at the office: her wedding ring. Eager to go home ever since her arrival, she now tells the nurse with good-natured irony, "It's been awfully nice, but I really *must* go."

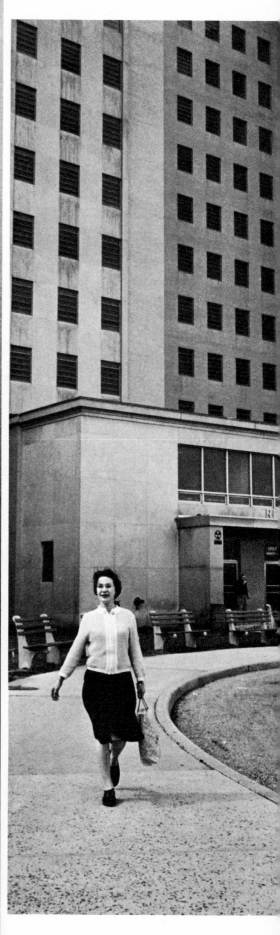

4

Psychoanalysis: Delving into the Unconscious

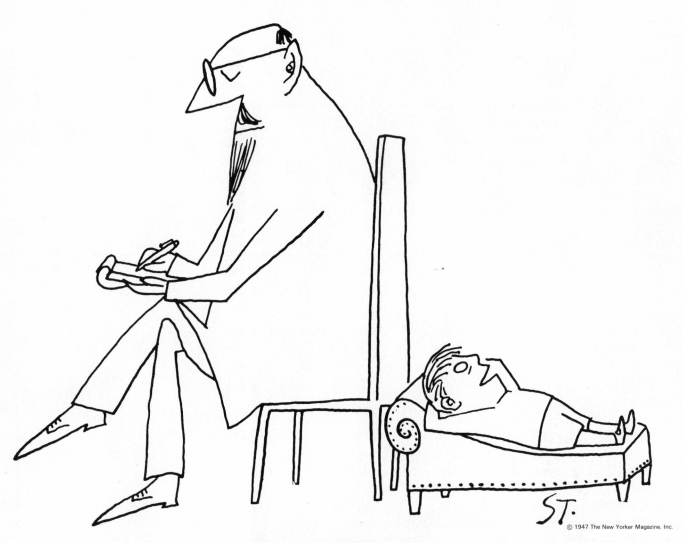

HARDLY EVER TOO YOUNG
This sardonic cartoon by Saul Steinberg shows a small boy being psychoanalyzed. When this cartoon appeared, less than 50 years after Freud launched his psychoanalytic method, Americans by the thousands were undergoing analysis. Analysts specializing in the treatment of children sometimes had patients as young as two.

THE MOST ORIGINAL THINKER in the field of human psychology was Sigmund Freud, the founder of psychoanalysis. Freud carefully constructed a doctrine of the mind which he developed over years of research and clinical investigation. He theorized that the mind operated on two levels, the conscious and the unconscious. From his findings that human urges and desires (many of them sexual in origin) existed primarily on the unconscious level, Freud developed a theory of personality which has deeply influenced all contemporary thought about the human mind and man's emotional life.

Popular interpretations of Freud's views have often distorted or oversimplified them. Among professionals, many psychologists and psychiatrists regard his theories with skepticism. Many psychoanalysts have departed from Freud's original doctrines, with the result that a number of schools incorporating modifications of Freudian principles have arisen during the last 20 or 30 years.

The climate of controversy, the diversity of interpretation which have always surrounded Freudianism and its metaphorical language combine to make it a confusing subject for the layman. One major obstacle to understanding the doctrine is that it demands acceptance of some ideas regarding human behavior which are distasteful to most people. An added difficulty is that Freud's theories are not open to the clear-cut confirmation or disproof required by the normal scientific method, even though he built his theories and techniques on experiences gained in treating patients for certain psychological disorders. Though it would be logical, therefore, to expect that his theories could be checked against the results they produced, a number of factors make this impossible. For one thing, treatment by psychoanalysis is so time-consuming that the possibility always exists that a patient's difficulties may simply disappear over the long time span, just as some physical ailments do. It is also possible that the close personal attention given to a patient during analysis might in itself be responsible for certain desirable changes in his attitude and behavior, regardless of whether the analytic theories are valid or not. These possibilities, plus the large number of other variables in every therapeutic situation, make controlled scientific experimentation extremely difficult in this field. So nobody has yet produced irrefutable evidence, one way or the other, regarding the validity of the Freudian hypotheses embodied in psychoanalysis.

Nevertheless, Freud's mark is on the world all around us. We cannot escape it. Terms like "repression" and "Oedipus complex" are part of our vocabulary. Many authors have been profoundly affected by Freud's teachings and it is now almost impossible to avoid his influence in books, plays, movies, poetry and ballet. In social relationships, in assessment of international conduct, or in dealing with the mentally ill we often employ a Freudian approach. Even those who attack Freud and impugn his beliefs frequently find themselves using his phraseology. Freud was unquestionably one of the most important men of his time. What sort of a man was he? And what did he really say? And how did he come to say it?

Sigmund Freud was born in 1856 in a small town in Moravia, then part of the Austrian Empire. He lived almost his whole life in Vienna until he left for London in 1938. There he died the following year.

A brilliant student, Freud had no clear idea of where his main interests were to lie when he left secondary school. After some deliberation, he registered as a medical student at the University of Vienna. Subsequently, he entered clinical medicine in order to earn a living—and found a new interest in the disorders of the nervous system. The facilities for pursuing neurology were limited in Vienna in 1885, and Freud went to Paris. There he studied under Jean-Martin Charcot, a famous teacher and one of the most eminent neurologists of his day. Charcot's specialty was the investigation of hysteria. Freud was particularly interested in this aspect of Charcot's work because the Frenchman used hypnosis to remove hysterical symptoms in patients.

Hypnosis for catharsis

Freud was already aware of hypnosis. Josef Breuer, a fellow physician in Vienna, had experimented with hypnosis in treating various nervous disorders. Under Charcot's tutelage Freud came to believe still further in the possibilities of hypnosis. He watched Charcot successfully convince a patient in a hypnotic trance that his hysterical symptom would vanish when he awoke. Charcot could also induce hysterical symptoms in a healthy person who was under hypnosis.

On his return to Vienna, Freud and Breuer collaborated in using hypnosis. Their use of the hypnotic state went much farther than Charcot's. While a patient was in a hypnotic trance, they encouraged him to talk freely about his emotional stresses. This process of revealing the hidden stresses was called "catharsis." Freud believed it had therapeutic value when and if the patient relived his true emotions, purging himself of them in the process.

In 1893 the doctors wrote a preliminary paper indicating the results of their investigations. This was expanded into a book, *Studies in Hysteria*, which was published in 1895, the year after their collaboration ended.

One of the basic elements of Freudian doctrine was the importance he placed on neuroses. He defined neurosis as the faulty resolution of a conflict between an individual's drives and his efforts to keep these urges and impulses from reaching the conscious level. For example, a man may be neurotically timid because he lives with a deep-rooted hostility against authority which he never dares to acknowledge consciously.

Though he was able to treat some neuroses successfully with his initial analytic technique of hypnosis and catharsis, Freud found that many cases resisted treatment. He finally concluded that in order to treat these cases successfully an analysis in much greater depth would be necessary, one that went as far back as childhood. Freud had long been impressed by the number of his patients who remembered sexual experiences in childhood. Many neurotic women claimed they had been sexually assaulted, often by their fathers or brothers. When Freud investigated, he found that many of these stories could not be confirmed and were almost certainly spurious. As he saw it, these memories could only be sexual fantasies which had arisen early in life. Eventually, this led him to the startling twin conclusions that neuroses originated in childhood and that they were predominantly sexual in nature.

In the decade after his break with Breuer, Freud developed his theories on the importance of infantile sexuality. As might be expected, he encountered great resistance in all quarters when he published his book, *Three Contributions to the Theory of Sex*, in 1905. But he persisted with his theory, and it became the basis on which he built the rest of the elaborate doctrine which now bears his name. Freud always insisted that anyone who wished to practice psychoanalysis had to accept as a fundamental his views about the role of sex in personality disorders.

Freud's doctrines, which he developed gradually, were ambitious and comprehensive. Built up piece by piece over the course of his long career, they were often modified in the light of later experience and observation.

Essentially, he was concerned with the emotions rather than the intellect. In fact, one of the most important aspects of Freudian theory is the role assigned to emotion and unconscious motivation, rather than intelligence, as the prime movers of our lives. This was shocking to people who believed that man was, above all, a rational being. Freud did not invent the concept of the unconscious, but he was the first to insist that studies of the mind could not be limited simply to the realm of the conscious. Indeed, one of Freud's major conclusions was that the unconscious psychic life was far more important than the conscious.

Harbor of the unconscious

This emphasis on the unconscious was one of Freud's most creative contributions to the problem of understanding how the personality harbors wishes and impulses which the conscious mind disavows. The rejected desires include all kinds of hostile and destructive impulses, as well as desires for proscribed forms of sexual gratification—all of which the conscious self of a civilized human being finds thoroughly distasteful to acknowledge. Awareness of these socially unacceptable desires and impulses arouses anxiety. To relieve the anxiety, impulses are blocked out of the consciousness by a process Freud called "repression." Even repressed impulses continually strive for expression and gratification, and thus exert a strong, lasting influence on the personality.

Freud held that an individual generally finds it impossible to give an account of the contents of his unconscious without guidance and assistance from a psychiatrist. The individual cannot describe these impulses, but they do appear, in disguised symbolic form, in his dreams, in slips of the tongue and lapses of memory. They also manifest themselves in overly emotional reactions, such as excessive remorse or apprehension. The mind resorts to various defenses in trying to prevent repressed desires from forcing their way into consciousness. One of these defenses is known as "reaction formation." An unconscious drive may show up in consciousness as its antithesis: thus reaction formation may lead to unconscious hostility being expressed as an exaggerated tenderness or regard. Another mechanism is "projection," in which an unconscious, unacceptable impulse is attributed to someone else in order to deny the impulse in oneself. For example, a person with a strongly repressed desire to steal will suspect those around him of being undetected thieves.

A third mechanism, "conversion," is found in hysteria. Here the conflict is converted into the symptom of a physical illness. In a case of conversion made famous by Freud, a young woman went out for a long walk with her brother-in-law, with whom she had fallen in love. Later, on learning that her sister lay gravely ill, she hurried to her bedside. She arrived too late and her sister was dead. The young woman's grief was accompanied by sharp pains in her legs. The pain kept recurring without any apparent physical cause. Freud's explanation was that she felt guilty because she desired the husband for herself, and unconsciously converted her repressed feelings into an imaginary physical ailment. The pain struck her in the legs because she unconsciously connected her feelings for the husband with the walk they had taken together. The ailment symbolically represented both the unconscious wish and a penance for the feelings of guilt which it engendered.

Clues to mental conflict

One of Freud's basic techniques for dealing with the unconscious developed out of the inadequacies he found in the use of hypnosis. Some of his patients could not be hypnotized at all, and even when hypnosis was successful, the cures he achieved were often only temporary. He began searching for an alternative approach to the unconscious. Gradually he developed a technique known as "free association." Patients were asked to relax on a couch and talk about whatever they liked—however absurd, inconsequential or even shocking it might sound. Freud found that he could trace powerful emotional drives and the sources of mental

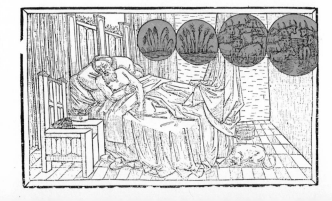

conflict in these sequences of a patient's seemingly confused thoughts.

Freud was quick to learn that free association sometimes resulted in a patient's remembering and describing a dream. He also found that these dreams could give him, as a doctor, valuable clues to a patient's inner feelings that produced psychological disorder. Finally Freud came to believe that dreams provided reliable and explicit information about a person's unconscious. There remained, however, the problem of interpreting the dreams as they were remembered and related. Since dreams are constructed of symbols that often seem totally illogical, Freud approached the problem of interpreting these symbols by dividing dreams into two constituent parts. In retelling the events that take place in a dream, a person provides the "manifest" content of the dream. The analyst attempts to interpret the symbolism of the manifest content and arrive at a more logical story. This then becomes the "latent"—the true, hidden—meaning of the dream. The latent content represents very often a desire to fulfill an unconscious wish too frightening or unpleasant or socially impossible to be allowed into consciousness—even in a·dream. The use of the free-association technique proved valuable in interpreting dream symbolism and in leading the analyst from the manifest to the latent content of the dream and consequently to its true significance. For example, Freud found that dreams of persons in authority, such as kings, governors or teachers, often symbolized the dreamer's parent and that is why a person might dream that he disobeyed a king.

Two vital instincts

For some time Freud believed that most neuroses are caused by the lack of a "normal" sexual life. Moreover, in Freud's view, sexual life does not begin at puberty but starts soon after birth. He pointed out that the drives of the sexual instinct (which Freud called the "libido") could be satisfied by many different activities and objects.

Initially Freud held that there were two vital human instincts—the drive toward self-preservation and the drive toward sexual gratification. The self-preservation drive takes care of the body, and since thwarting this drive for too long results in death, it is of little significance in the life of the individual. The sexual drive, or libido, on the other hand, is frequently repressed because of the forces of society upon the individual. This leads to changes in personality and in severe cases to some form of mental illness, such as a neurosis.

World War I stimulated Freud to develop still further this theory about psychological drives. Horrified by the carnage and destruction, he struggled to explain the obvious aggressive drives in the human character. He now felt there had to be another basic urge, a self-destructive one which he called the "death instinct." The two instincts of self-pres-

FREUDIAN DREAM SYMBOLS
Dreams, according to Freud, are repressed thoughts presented in a symbolic language *(below)*. A king, for example, might symbolize father. (Americans may dream of a President instead.) Being pulled from the water symbolizes birth, which Freud termed "the first experience attended by anxiety." A train represents death—missing a train means escape from death. Boxes indicate a desire to return to the womb.

FATHER

BIRTH

DEATH

WOMB

85

ervation and sexual gratification Freud now combined into one urge, the "life instinct," which he named "Eros." The life instinct was capable of diverting the death instinct away from the individual concerned and toward others in the form of outward aggression.

Freud began to elaborate his view of the personality after detailed observations of battle-shocked soldiers. In his modified interpretation of the instincts, he now went on to suggest that the personality was constructed of three parts. These he named the "id," "ego" and the "superego." This division has now become an integral part of Freudian theory.

The id is the wholly unconscious component of the personality, and is made up of primitive urges and instincts which seek gratification without regard to the consequences. The ego, in contact with the external world, stands between the id and the real world, and mediates the competitive necessities of the two. The superego is Freud's third component of the personality. Partly unconscious, the superego involves the inner acceptance of social values and ideals, and judges between good and bad behavior. Obedience to the superego promotes a feeling of self-esteem, while disobeying it produces guilt.

Transfer of hostility

Freud's psychoanalytic system was not simply a theory of the personality and its development; it was also the basis for a method of treating mental illness. In mediating the conflicting demands of the superego and the id, the ego can be damaged, and its owner will develop a neurosis. If the damage is limited, the person will continue to function but on a limited basis. When the ego loses its battle and can no longer function effectively, psychosis results. Psychotics generally revert to an infantile form of behavior and lead a simple, almost animal existence.

The technique of psychoanalysis helps the patient to discover what is going on within the unconscious depths of his mind, assists in the unraveling of the various conflicts and brings them to light within the conscious, where they can be dealt with more effectively. However, Freud learned from experience that simply being aware of a conflict was not enough, so he turned to the process of transference—and here the emphasis remains to this day among Freudian analysts. Suppose, for example, a patient had repressed a violent resentment toward his father. In analysis, the patient transfers the hostility he felt for his father to the analyst, who observes without uttering disapproval or criticism. Thus encouraged, the patient reveals his true, hidden feelings to the analyst, who can then guide him in understanding the original relationship with his father. Once the patient understands the original relationship—the source of his feelings of hostility—he no longer feels hostile either toward his father or toward the analyst.

MURDEROUS OEDIPUS

The woodcut above depicts a scene from the Greek legend of Oedipus, from which Freud took the term "Oedipus complex." Here Oedipus, who was abandoned in infancy, kills his father, a stranger to him, during a roadside argument. Later, still unaware of the relationships, he marries his father's widow, his mother. Freud believed this legend expressed a hostility to fathers that is felt by all sons.

Like many revolutionary doctrines, Freud's view of the mind first met with hostility and ridicule, but it did attract a small and enthusiastic group of followers. Later many of these found they were unable to accept all his doctrines and developed their own theories of human character. The most prominent were Alfred Adler and Carl Gustav Jung.

Alfred Adler began his medical career in Vienna in ophthalmology, then took up general practice before turning to psychiatry. Before he met Freud, Adler had developed certain psychological theories of his own. The most well-known of these today concerns the sense of inferiority. At first it seemed possible to regard the sense of inferiority as an extension of the ego function in Freudian theory. Adler developed his theory beyond Freud and believed that striving for superiority and the urge for self-realization were the most important influences on the personality. The search for sexual gratification, Adler held, was subsidiary to this drive for self-realization. Obviously, this conflicted with Freud's view of the fundamental importance of sexual drives, and a break with Freud became inevitable. Adler went on to develop not only his own psychological theory, with its now famous concept of the inferiority complex and its resulting compensation, but also his own methods of treatment.

Adlerian psychology assumes that man is motivated chiefly by social urges, and that the main driving force behind his actions is an innate desire for superiority. This may appear in a variety of different ways, and each individual selects his own "style of life," as Adler called it, in striving to develop and perfect his personality.

Compensating for inferiority

The style of life in Adlerian theory is formed early in childhood and alters little afterward. It is the result of an individual's reaction to his physical characteristics and to the influences exerted on him by his environment. Adler held that the role of a person's existence was hereafter arranged to accord with his style of life and governed his subsequent behavior. The individual's feelings of inferiority and his efforts to compensate for them largely determine what type of style of life he has. One example of compensation is provided by the career of Napoleon. In developing a style of life, according to this idea Napoleon compensated for his inferior size by dominating other people, then a whole nation and finally almost a continent—thus demonstrating, with a vengeance, his superiority. Today this need to compensate for being small by dominating others is popularly called the "Napoleonic complex."

Later Adler conceived a more dynamic principle, called the "creative self," whereby man constructs his individual personality out of his heredity and experience. It became the operating principle of life and may be likened to the spiritual concept of the soul.

ANXIETY

Contemporary artist Boris Artzybasheff portrays modern man's state of mind in this symbolic portrait called *Anxiety*. Here threatening faces, fangs and grasping hands menace the subject. According to Freud, anxiety may be caused by real danger, but when the danger is imaginary or unreasonably magnified, the anxiety is symptomatic of illness.

According to Adler's theory, the neurotic is a person who has failed to make a realistic adjustment between his desire for self-realization and the pressures of the society in which he lives. The neurotic's style of life, characterized by an extreme inferiority complex, often leaves him, for example, unable to make decisions. To Adler, sex represented only one of the problems an individual must solve. For, in Adlerian thinking, the style of life is settled before sexual problems appear during adolescence. Consequently it governs an individual's reaction to sex.

Adlerian analysis uses techniques similar to Freud's, including the analysis of dreams to determine a patient's style of life and the factors responsible for it in childhood. The treatment is shorter than Freudian analysis, since Adler did not wait passively to find out the basis of his patient's conflicts. Adler preferred a more direct, conversational approach, and even discarded the analyst's couch.

Adler's theory has the advantage of a certain down-to-earth simplicity, and there are few who would disagree that his main concept expresses an important truth about the source of many human attitudes. Yet his method, taken as a complete system, is not especially popular today, for it fails to explain far too many aspects of the mind, and many of his generalizations are regarded as superficial and implausible. Adler's influence on psychology has, nevertheless, been considerable, particularly in the field of child psychology.

Extroverts and introverts

Adler was open to criticism on the grounds of oversimplification. The other famous name associated with Sigmund Freud was Carl Gustav Jung, who had a deep interest not only in psychology but also in religion, symbolism, myths and metaphysics. Jung's brand of psychology emerged as a very complex doctrine. However, one of Jung's earlier works discussed in some detail the now familiar concepts of the introverted and the extroverted individuals—one of his most lasting contributions to psychology. It is perhaps ironic that the idea of people being introverts or extroverts—characterizations that are commonly used—should have come from a man whose other concepts were so complex and involved.

Jung's writings on the unconscious are both metaphysical and abstruse. He visualized the unconscious as existing in several layers, of which the most superficial is the personal unconscious. This resembles Freud's unconscious except that it also contained, besides material repressed from consciousness, other forgotten material.

In Jung's view, however, there were several other systems in the personality. One of these was the collective unconscious, which he regarded as the reservoir of latent memory-traces from all of man's past. Divorced from anything personal in the individual and common to all human beings, the collective unconscious was the inherited foundation of all personality. The ego and the personal unconscious were erected upon it. He claimed all our potential inclinations, our latent fears and desires came from the collective unconscious, and our experiences of the world were very largely shaped by it.

Another idea originated by Jung was the archetype. Part of the collective unconscious, archetypes were universal concepts containing a large element of emotion. For example, the shadow archetype consisted of the animal instincts inherited by man in his evolution from the lower forms of life. Jung considered it caused the appearance of behavior which is frowned on by society.

From Vienna, 1900, to the U.S., 1940

Contradictory though it may seem, Jung did believe in the validity of religious experience. And his system, or psychology, has derived its popular support from those who are repelled by the sexuality and materialism of Freud and who insist there must be a place for spiritual experience and religious belief.

The systems of Jung and Adler represent the two major offshoots from the main stream of psychoanalysis during Freud's lifetime. Since then there have been many modifications and extensions of the Freudian system.

In England, Anna Freud has developed her father's theories concerning the nature of the ego and its functions, and works extensively in child psychology. In the United States, the most important modifications of Freud's teachings came from Erich Fromm, Karen Horney and Harry Stack Sullivan. These neo-Freudians have attached far greater importance to interpersonal relationships and social environment. One of Horney's most interesting concepts was that of the importance of "hidden" values and desires. She made the point that Freud overemphasized sex, but agreed that sex was a dangerous topic for discussion in polite Viennese society at the turn of the century. However, in the United States of 1940, Karen Horney felt this was no longer true and that Freud's overwhelming emphasis on hidden sex impulses was out of date. She believed that concealing *any* desire or feeling was a more important factor than repressed sex. And she felt that these hidden wishes must be different in each age and each culture. She accepted the traditional analysis of the hidden desires in Viennese neurotics, but claimed that Freud was wrong in presuming that these must be the same in every society in every era. By placing less importance on sex, she helped to make Freudian analysis more acceptable to the general public.

Harry Stack Sullivan was one of the few in the analytic tradition who made a study of psychoses. He is particularly well known for his

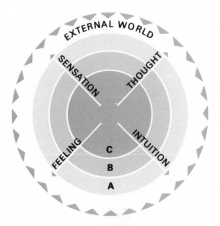

JUNG'S "MAP" OF THE MIND
Attempting to describe the "layers" of the human mind, Carl Jung went beyond the concepts used by Freud. To Freud's conscious (A), the part that deals with the external world, and unconscious (B), Jung added the "collective unconscious" (C). This innermost section, Jung said, holds the memories of all humanity and contains the roots of the four psychological functions: thought, intuition, feeling and sensation.

work in schizophrenia and for his theories concerning pathological thinking in this form of mental disorder. He took the view that the therapist should be especially sensitive to and aware of the problems of the schizophrenic, and attempt to understand the peculiar behavior and thinking patterns of the patient, bizarre though they may seem.

Freudian thinking together with its offshoots today dominates psychiatry, even though orthodox psychoanalysis has practical limitations as a universal method of treatment. Freudian therapy requires a generous expenditure of time and money, plus a degree of intelligence and cooperation on the part of the patient. These requisites are available only in a minority of cases.

Opinions still differ as to the validity of psychoanalysis. Experimental psychologists, with their emphasis on scientific proof, tend to regard the theory as inspired speculation rather than as a body of knowledge supported by solid evidence. The analysts reply that their critics misinterpret the theory and, moreover, insist on standards of proof that are too rigid for the difficult problems attacked daily by psychiatry.

Whatever the merits of these arguments, the Freudian view has had sufficient plausibility to survive vigorous onslaughts for more than half a century. Like many other forms of healing, it can boast spectacular successes—while critics continue to find an embarrassment of failures.

A Photographic Album from the Life of Sigmund Freud

Sigmund Freud unlocked a door in men's minds, explored the astounding chamber of the unconscious beyond, and redrew man's picture of himself. He had many of the bristling exterior traits that sometimes accompany greatness. Reserved and tenacious, he *knew* he was right and expected everyone to agree with him. He was often at odds even with disciples and colleagues. Yet, the sweetness of his personal life was disarming—and totally at variance with the irrational impulses he studied. The setting of his work was simple to an extreme. All his research was done with private patients in his Vienna consulting room. His happy marriage lasted 53 years; when he was away from home he wrote his wife daily. His life, as a son and as a father, was spent in large patriarchal families who took long summer vacations and lived in overfurnished rooms. He shaped the thinking of 20th Century man while remaining serenely 19th Century himself to the last.

PORTRAIT OF A POSITIVE MAN

Freud was 64 at the time of this portrait, made in 1920, but his theories of the unconscious were just beginning to find wide acceptance. By this time he had lost a number of followers because of his unyielding convictions, yet he was bitterly hurt when he aroused controversy, and never quite forgave the world for refusing to believe in his theories of the unconscious at the start.

Freud's birthplace, Freiberg, Moravia, is now in Czechoslovakia.

FAMILY PORTRAIT

An 1876 photograph of the Freuds includes 20-year-old Sigmund, then a medical student at the University of Vienna *(back row center, full-face)*, his parents *(seated)*, sisters, a brother and cousins. Sigmund was by now the undisputed eldest; his half-brother Philipp had left home.

WEDDING DAY PORTRAIT

Freud married Martha Bernays in 1886 after a four-year engagement. The young physician, wishing to support a family, had abandoned a career in physiological research to enter private practice as a neurologist. He spent the four years gathering clinical experience in preparation.

A Circle of Love and Hate

Freud once wrote, "The indisputable favorite of his mother keeps for life the feeling of a conqueror." Sigmund, born with "a lucky head of black hair," was the first of Amalia Freud's eight children, and she spoke often of his future greatness. But the boy's relationships to the men in his family were more complicated. Growing up in Vienna, Sigmund much admired his father, Jakob, who was old enough to be the child's grandfather. But Jakob had a son, Philipp, by a previous marriage, some 20 years Sigmund's senior, whom Sigmund resented.

Years later, after Freud had married *(opposite)*, he embarked on a crucial self-analysis. He discovered that he had believed Philipp to be his father, and that jealousy of Philipp's relationship with his beloved mother caused his hostility. This supported his findings from many patients—that even children have a sexual life.

93

A CONVINCING DEMONSTRATION

The Parisian neurologist Charcot exhibits to fascinated colleagues a woman paralyzed by her mental disorder, but able to rise from her bed under the influence of hypnosis. Charcot's daring experiments in hypnotizing mental patients and relieving their symptoms attracted students like Freud from across Europe. Freud hung the lithograph above in his Vienna office.

FOUNDERS OF A MOVEMENT

Freud made a trip to the U.S. in 1909, at the invitation of G. Stanley Hall *(seated, center)*, president of Clark University, Massachusetts. The small coterie at Clark included *(standing)* analysts A. A. Brill, Ernest Jones, Sandor Ferenczi and, flanking Hall, Freud and C. G. Jung.

The Beginnings of Psychoanalysis

By the 1880s, the treatment of mental illness in the civilized world had benefited from a burgeoning of scientific knowledge, and had passed into the hands of medical specialists—psychiatrists and neurologists. But even progressive practitioners, puzzled by cases of no apparent physical disorder, believed "degeneration" of the nervous system might be a cause.

In 1885, in preparation for private practice as a neurologist, Freud went to Paris to study under the eminent Dr. Jean-Martin Charcot *(opposite)*. There he witnessed Charcot's extraordinary experiments in hypnosis. The discovery that symptoms of mental illness might be caused and relieved by the power of "ideas" alone finally committed Freud to the study of the mind. He wrote of Charcot to his fiancée, "No other human being has affected me in such a way."

He was aware that a Viennese physician, Josef Breuer *(left)*, was already using hypnosis to bring forth his patients' repressed thoughts—a "catharsis" that Breuer found brought relief. When Freud returned home, he too began using hypnosis and catharsis. The two collaborated on a book, *Studies in Hysteria*, published in 1895. Freud, however, concluded from his own cases that all repressed thoughts are sexual in nature. Breuer could not agree and broke with Freud before publication. Freud soon departed from Breuer in another respect—replacing hypnosis with his own technique of "free association," in which the patient talks at random, uninterrupted. Thus, at the time the book appeared, Freud alone was left to lead the new era of psychoanalysis.

AN EARLY COLLABORATOR
Josef Breuer developed with Freud an early form of analytic therapy, but became alarmed when female patients fell in love with him. Partly for this reason, he dropped the method.

Freud's study was his private sanctum.

A Revolution in a Quiet Room

The Freuds lived for more than 40 years in a comfortable second-floor flat which, for most of these years, included his office. The doctor's chief income was from his patients (his fee was high for the time—$8.10 an hour) and his consulting room *(right)*, the epitome of civilized taste, reflected the tenor of his life. His devoted wife saw to it that the household revolved around *"Der Papa."* Daily he rose at 7 and was ready for his first patient at 8. Sessions lasted exactly 55 minutes. He lunched with Martha and their six children, often slipped across the hall to the family rooms during the five-minute breaks between appointments. He dined after his last patient at 9, then retired to his study, where he wrote until 1 a.m. or later.

IRRESISTIBLE SELF-EXPRESSION
Freud's Vienna consulting room, hung with rugs and pictures, was a showcase for his collection of ancient art. As his fame grew, princesses, poets and philosophers came to lie on his plush couch and unfold their dreams, fantasies and memories. One patient described Freud during analytic sessions as "terribly frightening"—exclaiming, gesticulating and puffing on his cigar.

SON AND HUSBAND
Freud's 70-year-old mother joined her son and daughter-in-law on a vacation in 1905. Freud detested Vienna, but in the mountains he loved he relaxed, wore Tyrolean shorts. Martha and the children often left Vienna for the mountains in June, where Freud later joined them.

A Wholehearted Leisure

Except for his cherished summer vacations, Freud engaged in few leisure activities: Sunday visits to his mother, meetings with his small group of followers, known as the Vienna Psychoanalytic Society. Saturday nights were sacred, reserved for animated bouts of tarok, an old Viennese card game.

Summer holidays abroad, however, were planned well in advance. The family usually settled in an Alpine resort, from where Freud often made trips to Italy. There he would enthusiastically explore cities and towns, haunt museums and perhaps buy an antiquity. Martha, a poor traveler, rarely came along, but Freud almost always journeyed with a friend, a relative or, in later years, his daughter Anna—for the great man never learned to read a railway timetable.

FATHER AND SON
Freud, a kind, if busy, father, fished in the Bavarian Alps in 1901 with Ernst, youngest of his three sons. He was an ardent walker and had a positive passion for hunting wild mushrooms and flowers, about which he knew a great deal. However, he regularly got lost in the woods.

FATHER AND DAUGHTER
Freud and his daughter Anna, youngest and favorite of his six children, strolled in the Austrian Alps about 1912. In his later years, Freud became more dependent on Anna than on Martha. Anna nursed him during his last 16 ill years, now carries on his analytic work in London.

BEDEVILED BY MAGICIANS

A suspicious Freud rejects the chummy welcome of a sorcererlike figure in a magazine cartoon of the 1930s. Freud's detractors regularly tried to undermine the scientific basis of psychoanalytic theory and liken it to the occult in spite of Freud's careful documentation. Actually Freud had always been mildly superstitious and occasionally flirted with numerology.

AN UNEASY SUBJECT

Scowling impatiently, Freud sat for a bust by the Yugoslav sculptor Olem Nemon in 1931, a time when many honors began to accrue. When Freud's maid saw the bust, she said, "The professor looks too cross." "But I am cross," Freud replied. "I am cross with mankind." He claimed at that time: "The attitude of the world . . . is no friendlier than 20 years ago."

An Impress on a New Century

Freud's early work on the unconscious was denounced from the first by the Vienna Medical Society. After the appearance in 1899 of *The Interpretation of Dreams*, he was stigmatized as antireligious by organized religion and as a smut-peddling sorcerer by the popular press, which claimed his books taught only that innocent babies lusted after their parents. Max Graf, a former student, said of these years, "People believed him a crazy man who saw sex in everything. Ladies blushed when you mentioned his name." After World War I, the world seemed readier to accept the fact of sex—and scientists to accept the growing evidence which Freud and his followers accumulated to support psychoanalysis. In 1931, his 75th birthday was an occasion for tributes from around the world—one of them from the Vienna Medical Society. The 20th Century had by now acknowledged him as one of the greatest shapers of the modern mind.

AN EARLY TRIBUTE

This medallion, presented in 1906, honored Freud's 25 years of work at the University of Vienna. It was one of the few honors he received from the city where he lived for 79 years.

AN IRONIC FLAG
Shortly after the *Anschluss* in 1938, Freud's house, like many in Vienna, was draped with swastika bunting. Three months later, Freud left for London. The Nazis failed to note his death there. After the war his name was on a list of those to be killed after the invasion of England.

Flight— and Final Days

In 1937, Freud wrote to Albert Einstein, "War is inevitable." It was inevitable too that after the Nazis had invaded Austria the Gestapo would harass the Jewish doctor. Although he rejected religion as an illusion which man created to compensate for inadequacies, Freud had always "proudly acknowledged his Jewishness."

Thus on May 21, 1938, the Nazi police raided the Freud apartment, where Freud was recuperating from one of 33 operations he endured for cancer of the jaw. As the Brown Shirts confiscated passports, impounded money and rummaged through papers and belongings, "Freud stood by calmly," according to *The New York Times*, "reassuring his household."

It took the diplomacy of both England and the U.S. to persuade the Nazis to let the great man emigrate. Freud, in turn, had to be persuaded to leave by the British psychoanalyst Ernest Jones, who would later write Freud's definitive biography. (Freud's first response was, "This is my post.") Princess Maria Bonaparte, a former patient, paid the ransom the Nazis demanded, and in June 1938 Freud, Martha and Anna left for London.

Freud was honored in exile. He spent the last year of his life quietly, seeing patients, relatives and friends. He died September 24, 1939, having become, as W. H. Auden has written, "a whole climate of opinion."

EN ROUTE TO EXILE
Supported by Maria Bonaparte and William C. Bullitt, then U.S. Ambassador to France, Freud arrives in Paris *(left)* in 1938 on his way to London. The blackest day of his life occurred shortly before, when the Gestapo arrested— but soon released—his beloved daughter Anna.

NEAR THE END
The 82-year-old master *(opposite)*, seen here in his London study, reads the manuscript of his last book, *Moses and Monotheism*, completed soon after he arrived in England. He suffered terrible pain from cancer, but he refused all painkillers until near the end, when he took aspirin.

5

How and What Do We Learn?

"LET US SUPPOSE THE MIND TO BE, as we say, white paper void of all characters, without any ideas. How comes it to be furnished? Whence comes it by that vast store which the busy and boundless fancy of man has painted on it with an almost endless variety? Whence has it all the *materials* of reason and knowledge?"

In short, how do we learn? The question was propounded almost three centuries ago by England's great John Locke, and it still detains us. Indeed, the question has assumed a new urgency in recent decades, as the irresistible forward sweep of the sciences has imposed startling new demands upon the capacity of men to learn. It is not only that our inventory of formal knowledge now turns over so rapidly; what is perhaps more challenging is the quickening pace of change in our physical and cultural environment. The daily papers are full of references that would have been incomprehensible to a college graduate 10 years ago. There are new countries on the map, exotic new metals in existence, more new drugs than the doctors can keep up with, new games and dances, new household appliances, new principles of law and new taxes. Thus there is more than ever to learn—and thus more pressure than ever to learn about the learning process itself.

Writing in 1687, Locke was under the impression that he had answered the main question about this process. We learn, he said, from experience —i.e., from the testimony of our senses and from our reflections upon this testimony. Nowadays, this may seem to most people to be merely common sense, but in the 17th Century it was a controversial view. The prevailing view before Locke had been that human beings had all sorts of a priori knowledge about the universe they inhabited.

Today, different kinds of answers to Locke's question are being demanded. Here are some of the questions asked:

• If we learn from experience, what kinds of experiences are most conducive to learning?

• Why do some individuals learn so much faster than others, even though their experiences are at least superficially similar?

• Why are so many individuals able to learn immediately how a diesel engine works but unable to grasp the simplest concepts of economics?

• Why does some learning last for life while other learning is forgotten in a few days?

And beyond questions of this kind, which pertain to "intellectual," or "symbolic," learning, there are others about the basic process by which people acquire habits, skills, tastes, prejudices, etc. Psychologists define the term broadly, so that it covers this kind of learning too; in one definition, for example, learning is "modification of behavior as the result of experience."

Psychologists have come to these questions from all directions and

THE URGE TO LEARN
A reading class in a Joplin, Missouri, elementary school demonstrates the fact that most children enjoy the process of learning. This is a continuous process not confined to the schoolroom—almost everything humans do, from infancy throughout adulthood, is "learned." Nearly all animals are capable of learning of some kind, but man is by far the best learner of all.

have supplied a disconcerting variety of answers to them. It is nevertheless possible to identify two broad lines of approach. One line is primarily concerned with behavior as central to any understanding of the learning process. In their efforts to understand that process, some psychologists—the behaviorists—have concentrated on studying observable acts (including the act of speech), and have generally viewed learning as behavior modified in response to specific stimuli. In this view the entire process is essentially mechanical. On the other hand, some psychologists have found the essence of learning to be cognitive, and to involve an act of "knowing." In the history of learning theory, it is not always clear whether the behaviorists and the cognitive psychologists have really been disagreeing with one another or simply emphasizing different aspects of learning and employing different vocabularies. But for whatever reason, our knowledge of the learning process has progressed along two separate paths, and most of the men contributing to that progress are identified with one tradition or the other.

The most famous name in modern learning theory is that of a Russian physiologist, Ivan Pavlov, who studied the digestive system through experiments on dogs. Although his work is basic to behaviorist psychology, Pavlov never considered himself a psychologist; indeed, he often used the term as an expression of contempt for those who were concerned with subjective matters. Pavlov himself believed that anything calling itself a science had to be based on objective, measurable data and a materialistic view of the universe. Pavlov himself was cold and unbending in his manner, totally committed to his research and given to violent outbursts at anyone who interfered with it.

Dogs, bells and saliva

Pavlov received the Nobel Prize for his work on the digestive system in 1904, and then went on to study the nervous system. In his experiments on dogs, Pavlov had noticed that he could stimulate the flow of digestive juices not only by placing food in the dogs' mouths, but also by simply showing it to them. This proved to him that some psychic phenomenon was at work, a phenomenon whose intensity could be measured objectively by recording the amount of saliva secreted by the dogs.

In Pavlov's most famous experiment, a bell was rung just before powdered meat was squirted into a dog's mouth. At first, the dog did not salivate until it actually got the meat. After the relationship between the bell and the meat had been established, it salivated at the sound of the bell. Finally, Pavlov found that the dog would continue responding to the bell even if it was not followed by meat. At least, it would continue for a while. Eventually the dog would stop salivating at the sound of the bell unless the meat was offered with it periodically.

Pavlov called the response to the bell a "conditioned reflex" and he came to view "conditioning" as "the principle of learning." He developed a number of procedures for strengthening, weakening and extinguishing conditioned reflexes. In one experiment, for example, he first conditioned a dog to salivate when it saw a circle. Next, the dog was shown an ellipse but given no food. The dog soon learned to discriminate between the two shapes. But then it was shown a series of ellipses, each a bit more circular than the last. Finally, when the ellipses had become almost circular, the dog's behavior changed drastically; it began barking and baring its teeth, refused to take any of the meat powder offered it, and soon proved to have lost its previously conditioned reflexes.

Pavlov worked only on the digestive system. His followers, in Russia and elsewhere, extended the conditioned reflex to other involuntary physical functions. Among other things, they conditioned a change in the heartbeat. But some psychologists were also attempting to teach animals to act more purposefully. At about the same time as Pavlov, an American named Edward Lee Thorndike achieved some fame in this field. Thorndike, a precursor of the behaviorist movement, was interested in the objective study of stimuli and responses, as Pavlov was. However, as a psychologist he was not concerned with the physiological processes underlying the responses.

Mazes and boxes

Thorndike viewed learning as problem-solving. He was the forerunner of several generations of American psychologists who devoted themselves to studying the ways in which dogs, cats and rats worked their ways through mazes and out of boxes. In one famous Thorndike experiment in 1898, hungry cats were placed inside boxes. They were fed only after they had escaped. To escape, they had to release a catch over the front of the box. There were several different ways in which they could do this. The experiment showed that a cat would usually begin rather aimlessly, thrashing about in all directions, until it accidentally sprang the release. The second and third time it was in the box, its performance might not be any better. But at some point, it would seem to learn what it had to do, and thereafter it would be out of the box in only a few seconds.

More than 60 years after this experiment, its implications are still not entirely clear. Thorndike himself believed that the cat was learning, through trial and error, how to solve a particular problem. He viewed trial and error as a process by which learners developed mental associations, or "connections," that enabled them to solve problems. ("Learning," Thorndike once said, "is connecting.") His so-called Law of Effect held that any connection producing a satisfying state would

PAVLOV'S EXPERIMENTAL APPARATUS
Strapped in, ready to begin, one of Pavlov's famous dogs stands surrounded by the apparatus devised by the Russian scientist to test conditioned reflexes. Saliva, carried by a tube to a beaker, activated a lever connected to the pen beyond the screen at left. Each drop of saliva was registered by a squiggle on the revolving drum. The dogs evidently learned to enjoy their work, hopping up onto the platform without being asked.

tend to be repeated; e.g., the cat would tend to repeat whatever behavior had led it to get out of the box the previous time. What is unclear, however, is whether the cats he tested understood how their behavior was helping them to get out of the box and at their food.

Some later experiments, conducted with more sophisticated equipment and carefully photographed, suggest that the cats may have simply discovered that when they bumped into the release mechanism they were soon out of the box—but that they may not have realized which movement it was that had sprung the release.

The "building blocks" of learning

Given the difficulty of interpreting tests involving animals, it is natural to question the emphasis that students of learning have placed on them. The psychologists' answer is that in some ways tests of humans are even harder to interpret. Because humans have, and are accustomed to using, several different kinds of very complex intellectual equipment, it is often hard to tell which kinds they are using to solve a particular problem. Suppose, for example, we want to test the ability of an animal to learn the relationship between two different places that are separated by a path with many detours on it. A human animal retracing his course on the path might depend heavily on sophisticated memory aids: "twice to the left, then once to the right, then left again," and so on. A rat, with more limited resources, provides a better opportunity to study the simpler mechanisms used by animals to orient themselves in space (although, as we shall see, there are some problems of interpretation with rats too). To get at the "building blocks" of learning, psychologists want to know the simplest, the most fundamental skills that are used to solve any problem.

In the 1920s, the turn toward behaviorist psychology reached its most intense and dramatic phase in the U.S. This was the period in which the doctrines of that strange and contradictory American, John B. Watson, were influential and controversial, both in academic circles and among the lay public.

Watson was the first psychologist to call himself a behaviorist. He was influenced by Thorndike's work and in some ways by the pragmatic philosophy expounded by John Dewey, under whom Watson studied at the University of Chicago (although years later Watson remarked that he had never really understood what Dewey was talking about). He became a professor of psychology at Johns Hopkins University when he was 29, and 11 years later published his most important book, *Psychology from the Standpoint of a Behaviorist.*

It was Watson's view that the mind could not be studied scientifically and should, in effect, be ignored by psychologists. The only thing that

THE EDUCATION OF A RAT

These drawings illustrating an experiment show a rat learning what to do in a tough spot by both the trial-and-error method and by conditioning. Moments after a light is flashed, an electric current is applied to the part of the floor immediately beneath the rat. It soon learns by trial and error to leap the barrier to escape the shock. As the sequence is repeated, the rat learns to associate the pain with the advance warning light. This conditioning further changes its behavior: without waiting for the shock, it leaps when it sees the light.

RAT DOES NOT OBSERVE LIGHT COMING ON

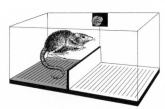

CURRENT ELECTRIFIES FLOOR, RAT JUMPS

could be studied scientifically was behavior. If we observed behavior closely enough, we could learn everything we had to about the mind. Though human beings were admittedly more complex than most other chunks of matter in this universe, they nevertheless responded predictably to outside forces. It was the ultimate aim of behaviorist psychology to be able to predict what the human responses would be if the stimuli were known.

How many emotions?

Watson contended that we are born with only three real emotions: fear of loud noises and of falling, anger at having our movements frustrated, and love at being petted or stroked. All other reactions, Watson said, are learned. He believed that he could teach children to avoid unreasonable fears and prejudices, and to behave rationally, by conditioning them at early ages. For some years, he worked at conditioning children. He experimented, for example, on eliminating their fears of animals by letting them see the animals while giving them at the same time something they liked to eat.

His essentially "mechanical" view of human beings led Watson into one controversy after another. Under his antagonists' goading—or in response to these stimuli, as a behaviorist might have described it—he was led into positions more extreme than those he had originally espoused. He warned repeatedly against excessive displays of affection in rearing children, but carried his argument on this issue to a point at which he seemed to be crusading against parental love in general. And he claimed a lot for his theories of child care. One famous pronouncement was: "Give me a dozen healthy infants, well-formed, and my own specified world to bring them up in, and I'll guarantee to take any one at random and train him to become any type of specialist I might select—doctor, lawyer, artist, merchant-chief, and yes, even beggarman and thief, regardless of his talents, penchants, tendencies, abilities, vocations, and race of his ancestors. I am going beyond my facts and I admit it, but so have the advocates of the contrary, and they have been doing it for many thousands of years."

Watson had an odd career. He was fired by Johns Hopkins in 1920, when his domestic difficulties, and ultimately his divorce, attracted a lot of publicity. Though his intellectual influence was probably at its height at this time, Watson did not resume his scholarly career; instead, he went into advertising. He continued to write and lecture on behaviorism, and to attract controversy. His views on rearing children were publicly attacked by his own son in 1950. But by 1958, when Watson died, much more sophisticated behaviorist theories on learning had been developed, and he is now regarded by psychologists not as a

ALERT RAT BEGINS TO NOTICE LIGHT

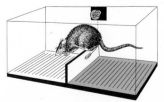

CURRENT ENTERS FLOOR AND RAT JUMPS

CONDITIONED RAT JUMPS AS LIGHT COMES ON

scholar but as a distinguished forerunner whose findings remain relevant.

Behaviorists before and after Watson investigated the learning process by studying stimuli and responses "atomistically"—that is, by breaking down the process into its basic elements so that cause and effect might be discerned more clearly. Thorndike's trial-and-error studies, too, were concerned with detailed analysis of behavior in learning. This kind of approach was challenged by the Gestalt psychological school when it became influential in the 1920s.

The Gestalt psychologists, who were plainly working in the cognitive tradition, believed that normal learning involved a process of organization that had to be studied as a whole—whence Gestalt, or "whole." In their view, learning could not be broken down into connections, for example, or conditioned reflexes.

Köhler's apes

One of the most influential of the Gestalt psychologists was Wolfgang Köhler, who developed a new theory of learning while studying anthropoid apes on the island of Tenerife, off the northwest coast of Africa. He had arrived there in 1913, as director of the Prussian Academy of Sciences' research station, and was stranded on the island when war broke out in 1914. Köhler made good use of the opportunity to develop his theories, which were later published in his famous book, *The Mentality of Apes.*

Köhler showed that apes normally solve problems in ways that suggest thought processes at work. One interesting side effect of his experiments was to settle, pretty conclusively, the age-old argument as to whether man was the only animal capable of reasoning. Attempting to reach food placed outside its cage and beyond its grasp, an ape would pick up a stick and manipulate the food into a more accessible position. The ape showed that it could devise its own tools, for example, when it broke off a branch in order to get at the food. In another famous experiment, Köhler placed two hollow bamboo rods inside an ape's cage. Neither of the rods was long enough to reach the food, but the ape pushed the narrower rod into the end of the other, forming one stick that *was* long enough. When fruit was placed above them and out of reach, the apes constructed a platform of boxes to get at it. The animals' approach to these problems, in short, was quite different from that of Thorndike's cats. Frequently, Köhler reported, an ape would sit looking at the problem for some time, and then seem to grasp the solution quite suddenly. Köhler declared that this was "insightful behavior."

The influence of the cognitive theorists has until recently been overshadowed by psychologists working in the behaviorist tradition. The rest of this chapter may profitably be given over to the findings of three

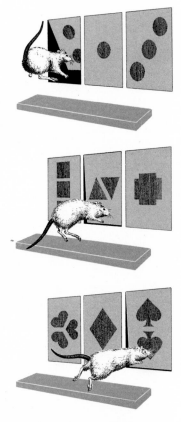

THE CONCEPT OF TWONESS

These pictures, based on an experiment at Tulane University, show a rat learning a skill formerly associated only with humans: grasp of the concept of "twoness." First the rat learns that his food lies through the door with two dots *(top).* Next, different shapes are substituted on the three doors, but in every case the way to the food is through a door with two figures *(center and bottom).* Twoness was a difficult lesson for the Tulane rat to learn, but after 1,500 trials it finally grasped the pure mathematics involved and was able to collect its reward every time *(right).*

extraordinary men: one a behaviorist, one a cognitive theorist, and the third more difficult to categorize. All three have put some new and startling propositions to educators.

The "rat psychologist"

The man difficult to categorize was Edward C. Tolman, who died in 1959. He cheerfully referred to himself as a "rat psychologist." In more than three decades at the University of California, he and his students almost certainly learned more from experimenting on rats than anyone would have dreamed possible in Thorndike's era.

Tolman was an imaginative and far-ranging psychologist, who had assimilated elements of Gestalt theory, Freudianism and other psychological schools into his own doctrine, which he called "purposive behaviorism." His reports on rat behavior were always immensely suggestive about human behavior as well. Most suggestive of all, perhaps, was his concept of "cognitive maps" in rats and men, which he put forward in 1948.

Tolman began his explanation of cognitive maps by dividing animal psychologists into two principal schools. One, composed of the more orthodox behaviorists, viewed the learning process of rats in mazes as a matter of strengthening some stimulus-response connections while weakening other connections. The other school, with which Tolman identified himself, believed "that in the course of learning, something like a field map of the environment gets established in the rat's brain. . . . Although we admit that the rat is bombarded by stimuli, we hold that his nervous system is surprisingly selective as to which of these stimuli it will let in at any given time." Instead of responding to all stimuli, Tolman argued, the rat worked them over in a "central control room," so to speak, until it had figured out "a tentative, cognitive-like map of the environment. And it is this tentative map, indicating routes and paths and environmental relationships, which finally determines what responses, if any, the animal will finally release."

Tolman made an important distinction between what he called "strip maps" and "comprehensive maps." An animal with a strip map in its head pursues a narrow and undeviating path in solving a problem. An animal with a comprehensive map has a more generalized view of matters, and may vary its procedure from one time to the next. Both maps, Tolman said, may serve to solve a particular problem. But when the problem changes somewhat, a narrow strip map proves useless, while a comprehensive map may enable the animal to adapt to the change.

Tolman found the concept of the cognitive map useful in explaining a variety of curious learning patterns observed in rats. For example, one group of experiments suggested that rats could redo a problem many times while apparently failing to improve their performances significantly. But when they began to receive a special incentive (e.g., a feeding when the problem was solved), they would improve dramatically. In fact, the improvement from that point on would be sharper than that of other rats who were just beginning to work on the problem and were also receiving the incentive. Thus there must have been some "latent learning" going on even when the rats' performance did not show it. "They had," Tolman concluded, "been building up a 'map,' and could utilize the latter as soon as they were motivated to do so."

Human beings are obviously better off if their own cognitive maps are comprehensive rather than strip maps. Tolman suggested that humans are apt to be handicapped by strip maps when their motivations are uncontrollably strong, or when they suffer from intense frustrations. "Over and over again," he wrote, "men are blinded by too violent motivations and too intense frustrations into blind and unintelligent, and in the end desperately dangerous, hates of outsiders. And the expression of these, their displaced hates, ranges all the way from discrimination against minorities to world conflagrations."

The behaviorist among these three men, B. F. Skinner of Harvard, is probably one of the best-known psychologists now active in the U.S. Like many famous scholars, he appears to have achieved fame for accomplishments that he considers secondary. His fame with the public rests principally upon his identification with teaching machines, as though he were the inventor of a new gadget. Actually he views the theory underlying the machines—i.e., his analysis of behavior—as a more important contribution to American education, and history may well prove his judgment correct.

Table tennis for pigeons

Like most modern behaviorists, Skinner lays great stress upon the concept of "reinforcement"—that is, strengthening a desired response through reward. This part of the theory is not original with Skinner, but he did push into new ground with the idea of breaking behavior down into many small components and reinforcing each of them systematically. In this way even complex behavior, including learning behavior, could be "shaped" by a teacher. Skinner has demonstrated these principles dramatically in experiments with pigeons. He has, for example, taught them to discriminate among playing cards, to peck out tunes on a toy piano, and even to play a kind of table tennis.

His ultimate interest, of course, has been human learning, and the possibility of shaping human behavior in ways that constitute learning. In the best behaviorist tradition, Skinner insists on defining learning only in relation to behavior: "We can define terms like 'information,' 'knowledge,' and 'verbal ability' by reference to the behavior from which we infer their presence. *We may then teach the behavior directly.* Instead of 'transmitting information to the student,' we may simply set up the behavior which is taken as a sign that he possesses information. . . ."

The practical application of this view of learning was the teaching machine. Several varieties of these have been devised by Skinner and others, but all work essentially in the same way. The machine shows the student a problem, typically in the form of a sentence to complete. When he supplies an answer, he can immediately see the right answer. If his own answer was correct, he is rewarded by a feeling of self-satisfaction, and so his behavior is reinforced. The student usually does, in fact, get the right answer, for it is an essential article of Skinner's doctrine that he be started off on very easy problems; in the course of mastering these he absorbs enough information to go on successfully to the hard ones. More conventional teachers sometimes ask tricky questions, expecting thereby to catch the careless student. But Skinner believes instead in getting the careless student into the habit of answering correctly, i.e., in reshaping his learning habits until he ceases to be careless.

Machines versus books

The teaching machine has some extraordinary advantages over conventional teaching methods. Its main one, perhaps, is that every student can push ahead at his own speed, without reference to what the rest of the class is doing; students who must review something over and over are perfectly free to do so, and other students are free to race through one program and go on to the next. Some schools that have tried teaching machines are enthusiastic about them. Other schools feel that the machines impose unnecessary constraints upon the scope and variety of the material to be taught; there are too many limits upon teaching through sentences-to-be-completed.

In any case, some feel that Skinner's doctrines may be implemented successfully—perhaps more successfully—without machines. What is fundamental to his doctrines is the programming of education, i.e., taking students a step at a time from the simple to the complex, while reinforcing learning. Several experiments are now being conducted to combine the programming concept with an old-fashioned teaching device: the textbook.

Skinner's work has an exciting pioneering quality about it, and so does the work of one of his colleagues at Harvard who is, however, pursuing a quite different approach to learning. The colleague is Jerome Bruner, codirector of the Center for Cognitive Studies at the university. Perhaps because he was born blind (he first saw, after an operation, when he was two years old), Bruner has always been fascinated by the nature of perception. He divides the phenomenon into three elements. In his view, perception begins with a "set," or hypothesis about what is to come—i.e., with "a highly generalized state of readiness to respond selectively to classes of events in the environment." This hypothesis is based on past experience. The second stage in perception is the input of information from the environment. The third state is the act of "checking," or confirmation. "If confirmation does not occur, the hypothesis shifts. . . ."

In teaching children, Bruner believes, it is important to get them to check their hypotheses carefully. Children have a natural tendency to jump to conclusions, and one of the signs of a maturing intelligence is a child's willingness to suspend judgment, to keep the hypothesis open, to keep the state of readiness generalized. Bruner considers the most important ingredient in learning to be "a sense of excitement about discovery—discovery of regularities of previous unrecognized relations and similarities between ideas, with a resulting sense of self-confidence in one's abilities." In order to enable the child to make this discovery, the material must be structured or presented in a way that is meaningful to him. Bruner has gone so far as to suggest, in an often-quoted statement, "Any subject can be taught effectively in some intellectually honest way to any child in any state of development." It is a dazzling vision.

Patterns of Learning, Levels of Ability

The preoccupied boy pictured on the opposite page is struggling to grasp a concept that will change his attitude toward numbers for life. In this he has a close kinship with the rat that learns to negotiate a simple maze. Psychologists define learning as any change in behavior as the result of experience. Lower animals follow many curious, unlearned, unchangeable ways we call instincts, but almost all can also learn to adapt their behavior to some extent. Scientists study the learning processes of animals like rats and monkeys in order to understand some of our own. But the capacity to learn increases directly with intelligence. Man, with his high intelligence, learns all he needs to know to survive, and keeps right on learning. His behavior is extraordinarily flexible; with his gift for words, he deals with a whole world of ideas. Some men go on to the highest feat of all: the creation of new ideas worth learning by the rest of us.

MIND AT WORK
Concentrating on a problem in arithmetic, a bemused boy works with an "addition strip board," developed in schools using Montessori teaching methods. The board's colored, removable strips represent the numbers from one to nine. Modern educational equipment such as this helps a child learn not only with his reasoning powers but also through sight, touch and physical motions.

FEAR IN DEPTH

The baby pictured above took an unhappy part in an experiment to find out when humans can perceive depth. Placed on a glass sheet several feet above the floor, he helped show that a baby old enough to crawl already has the visual capacity to recognize a drop. He not only saw the yawning space below, but his reaction proved he knew it was something to avoid.

SUSPICIOUS PIGLET
This pig, exploring the same glass table as that pictured opposite, reacted even faster than the baby when pushed out onto the glass. It either froze there in terror or backed up in a frenzy.

On the Threshold of Learning

It is a rule of thumb that the lower the animal, the more it depends on inborn ways of taking care of itself. Chicks, for example, start scratching for food a few hours after birth. Many lower animals depend on other instinctive behavior for the most important events of their lives, such as courtship and nest-building. Their ways of doing things are inflexible *(right)*, but often astonishingly elaborate.

Man has no innate fixed behavior patterns other than a few reflexes. He has, however, the best resource of all for dealing flexibly with all situations: a huge capacity for learning. And even though he makes a strikingly helpless newborn, he is alert to danger at an early age *(opposite)*.

BEARDED MOTHER GOOSE
German naturalist Konrad Lorenz found that at a critical time just after hatching, goslings instinctively follow the first large moving thing they see—normally their mother. In this case he presented himself and with their first fateful look in his direction, they followed.

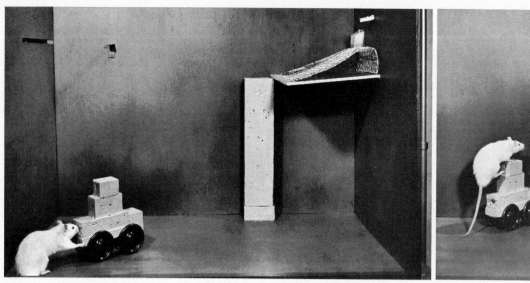

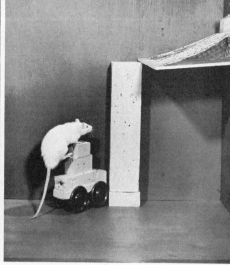

The rat looks as though it had used an intelligence akin to man's to figure out how to reach the cheese. Actually, experimenters taught it ea

Low-level Learning

Ever since man tamed his first wild creature, he has known animals can learn. He has been slower to admit that their learning processes are the same as some of his own. Countless experiments on animals in 20th Century laboratories, however, have shed light on how learning takes place —and have proved convincingly that man and animal share ways of learning below the level of reason.

Animals, for example, need a motive to learn, much as humans do. The cart-pushing rat shown above was guided to do its stunt with an incentive (cheese), much as parents guide children with punishments and rewards. The rat at right is discovering through its own experience (trial and error) where its reward lies, at the end of the maze.

A few smart animals, such as some monkeys and apes, learn to please by mimicry. But even they are not as good at imitating as human adolescents.

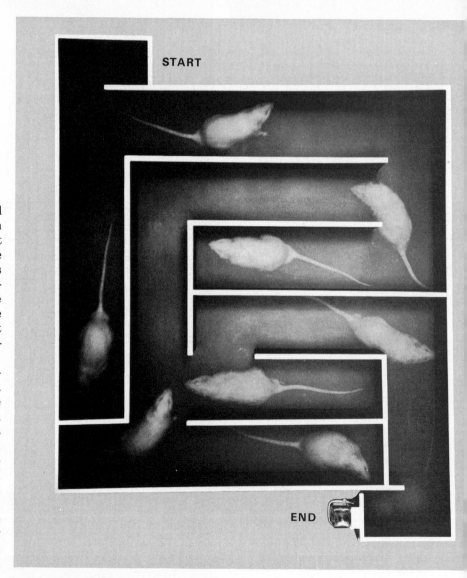

START

END

SHORTEST WAY HOME

A maze is a good test of an animal's ability to learn from trial and error. In the first of the two multiple-exposure pictures above, the rat is shown making all of the possible wrong turns it could make in negotiating the maze from start to finish. But finally, after six run-throughs,

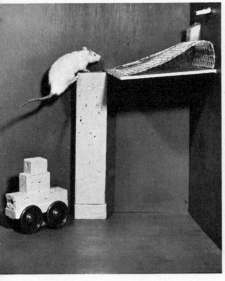

move separately, then to link them together. All the rat provided was eagerness for a reward.

LEARNING BY REWARD

Rats make good laboratory animals because they are quick to learn behavior associated with a reward. The rat pictured at left learned to push a cart—although pushing is unnatural for rats—to climb the tower and scurry up the ramp, because repeated experiences showed it such behavior was invariably associated with a morsel of cheese at the end of the sequence.

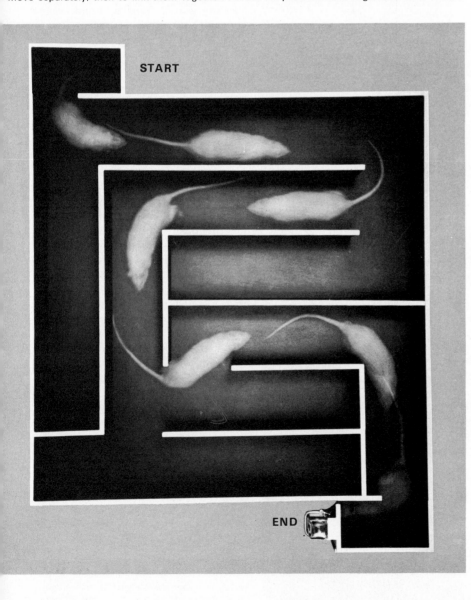

LEARNING BY IMITATION

Chimpanzees are among the smartest of all animals, and Zippy, who has played Cheetah in Tarzan movies, is smart enough to imitate quite elaborate behavior of others. This is often a route to useful learning, although in this case Zippy is only looking for the reward of attention.

the rat had learned the way without a mistake. The second picture shows it heading straight for its reward, a dish of water, at the end. Being a curious creature, a rat will sometimes go back to sniff around in an unvisited corner, but once it learns a maze it will remember it indefinitely.

The Priceless Gift of Language

Man, with his highly evolved brain, has the gift of language—and with this unique tool has opened up frontiers of learning sealed to all dumb animals. Words, those easily communicable, abstract symbols for everything visible and invisible he cares to think about, tumble in his brain and from his tongue: English is just one collection, but it consists of more than half a million of them. They are our flexible, almost inexhaustible currency of communication. They can be written, enabling us to communicate the whole body of our past as well as the present. Finally, they are the basic tools we think with. Every evidence indicates that without a knowledge of words, intellectual activity of all kinds is impaired.

Acquiring a language, then, is the first step to higher learning. Man starts the process remarkably young for an animal that matures as slowly as he does. A three-month-old baby can vocalize all the sounds he will need, and by about two begins to use words to convey meaning. By six he is ready to go to school—launched on the business of more formal learning.

THE WRITTEN WORD
Two Chinese boys in a school in Thailand come face to face with the mysteries of the written word. By the age of six, the normal human brain is so adept at handling symbols that what is no more than an arbitrary squiggle soon takes on meaning: in this case the word "rain."

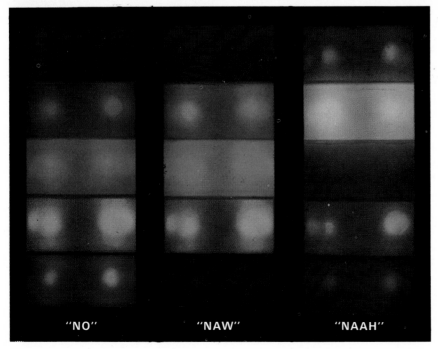

"NO"   "NAW"   "NAAH"

LEARNING TO SPEAK

Working hard to say "shoe" into a saucer-shaped microphone, a deaf girl *(above)* watches colored panels which tell her visually when she is making the right sound. Language is so important to humans that even the deaf eagerly try to learn it by one method or another.

SOUND MADE VISIBLE

The machine used by the deaf girl above is called a Chromalizer. It converts the sounds of words into color patterns. Since human speech is so infinitely varied, the machine must be extremely sensitive. The picture at left shows the color patterns made by three similar sounds.

Machines to Meet a Crisis

Man has increased both his population and his body of knowledge at a dizzying rate just within the span of a single generation. Now he faces a critical need for more people to learn more things than ever before. Inevitably, he is turning to machines to help him meet the crisis.

Teaching by machine may be regarded as a mixed blessing, but machines can unquestionably do things humans cannot. For example, they can deliver quantities of vivid sensory stimuli into the classroom as an aid to learning. Man possesses an enormous capacity for seeing, hear-

ing and storing information from all sides—a capacity barely touched by old teaching methods. Pictures, films and sound tracks now enable many students to gather impressions in a short time, and new ways of using the senses even more fully in learning are being developed (*above*).

The machine pictured at right, on the other hand, puts its students through learning processes as old as the one-room schoolhouse. It is no more creative than the material put into it by humans, but it offers one important advantage over good living teachers: it can be mass-produced.

MECHANICAL SCHOOLMARM
This typewriter-sized machine, the Didak, can be crammed with facts. An educator once described such machines as "the ideal teacher who always says the right thing at the right time, adjusts . . . the material to the . . . student, has endless . . . patience, and is never bored."

THEATRICAL CLASSROOM

Designer Ken Isaacs is seen inside *(left)* and in the door *(above)* of his "knowledge box." This strictly experimental device beamed pictures on the ceiling, walls and floor through the many square apertures visible in the large photograph, flooding an observer's mind with images.

CUSTOM-TAILORED BLACKBOARD

The tape showing in the window of a Didak *(below)* intersperses facts with sentences, which the student completes in the space provided. He actively participates, he moves at his own speed and knows at all times just how well he is doing—all ideal educational practices.

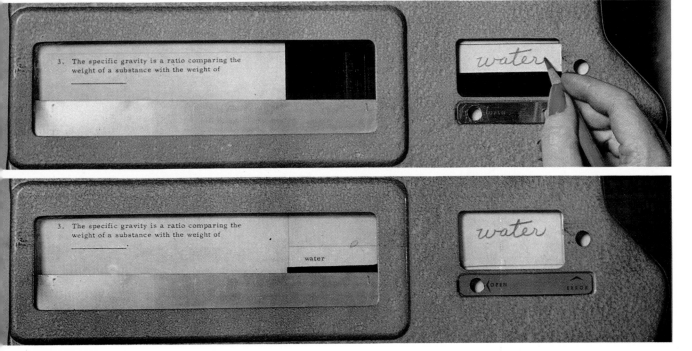

3. The specific gravity is a ratio comparing the weight of a substance with the weight of

_____

water

3. The specific gravity is a ratio comparing the weight of a substance with the weight of

_____

water

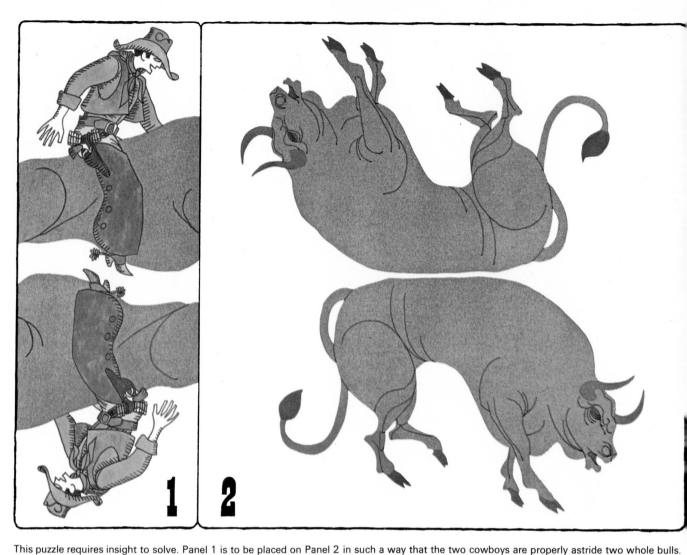

This puzzle requires insight to solve. Panel 1 is to be placed on Panel 2 in such a way that the two cowboys are properly astride two whole bulls.

THE CASE OF THE HIDDEN STAR
Somewhere in the mosaic above is a symmetrical, five-pointed star, like those in American flags. Solving this puzzle calls for persistent logic in the face of myriad visual distractions.

Tests of Intelligence

In 1904 a French psychologist, Alfred Binet, devised the first successful scientific test to measure human intelligence. What was it measuring?

Intelligence covers a broad range of mental activities, from insight to logical thought, and some of them can be tested by problems and puzzles like the two that appear on this page. But a true intelligence test, unlike the puzzles, evaluates the subject's intelligence with a score. Since Binet's time, many such tests have been designed and given to literally millions of people. Since all the aspects of intelligence seem to include a capacity for grasping intangible concepts, most, like the partial test on the opposite page, measure our ability to find meaning and relationship in pure concepts: words, numbers, geometric figures. They do not measure how much we know, or our motivation or persistence, all of which help determine our success at intellectual tasks. Deliberately impersonal as they are, though, they reliably measure a capacity we use in personal ways to enrich our lives. (Test and puzzle answers are on page 193.)

SAMPLE INTELLIGENCE-TEST PROBLEMS

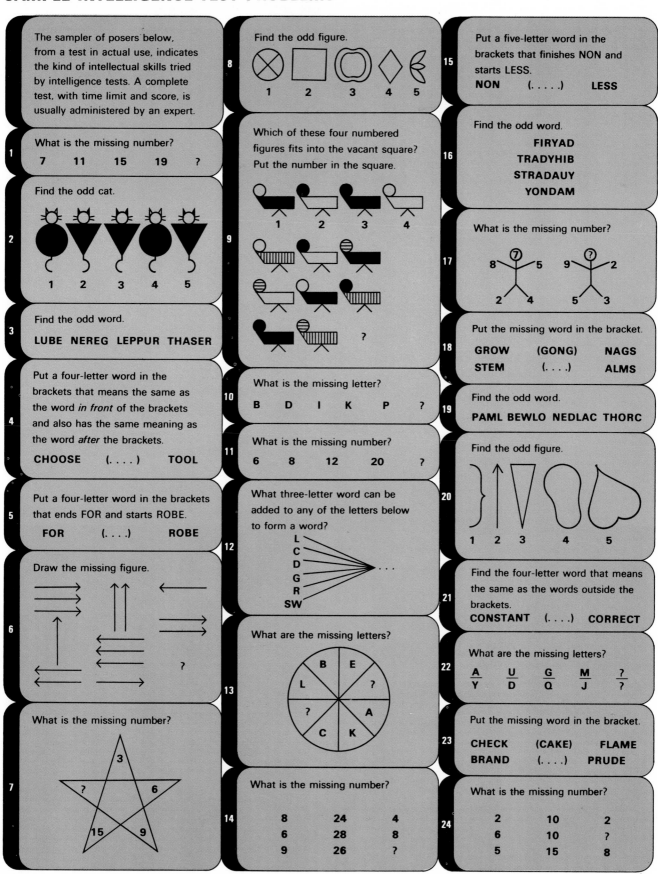

The sampler of posers below, from a test in actual use, indicates the kind of intellectual skills tried by intelligence tests. A complete test, with time limit and score, is usually administered by an expert.

1 What is the missing number?

7   11   15   19   ?

2 Find the odd cat.

1   2   3   4   5

3 Find the odd word.

LUBE   NEREG   LEPPUR   THASER

4 Put a four-letter word in the brackets that means the same as the word *in front* of the brackets and also has the same meaning as the word *after* the brackets.

CHOOSE   (. . . .)   TOOL

5 Put a four-letter word in the brackets that ends FOR and starts ROBE.

FOR   (. . . .)   ROBE

6 Draw the missing figure.

7 What is the missing number?

8 Find the odd figure.

1   2   3   4   5

9 Which of these four numbered figures fits into the vacant square? Put the number in the square.

10 What is the missing letter?

B   D   I   K   P   ?

11 What is the missing number?

6   8   12   20   ?

12 What three-letter word can be added to any of the letters below to form a word?

L
C
D
G   . . .
R
SW

13 What are the missing letters?

14 What is the missing number?

8   24   4
6   28   8
9   26   ?

15 Put a five-letter word in the brackets that finishes NON and starts LESS.

NON   (. . . . .)   LESS

16 Find the odd word.

FIRYAD
TRADYHIB
STRADAUY
YONDAM

17 What is the missing number?

8 ⑦ 5   9 ? 2

2   4   5   3

18 Put the missing word in the bracket.

GROW   (GONG)   NAGS
STEM   (. . . .)   ALMS

19 Find the odd word.

PAML   BEWLO   NEDLAC   THORC

20 Find the odd figure.

1   2   3   4   5

21 Find the four-letter word that means the same as the words outside the brackets.

CONSTANT   (. . . .)   CORRECT

22 What are the missing letters?

$\frac{A}{Y}$ $\frac{U}{D}$ $\frac{G}{Q}$ $\frac{M}{J}$ $\frac{?}{?}$

23 Put the missing word in the bracket.

CHECK   (CAKE)   FLAME
BRAND   (. . . .)   PRUDE

24 What is the missing number?

2   10   2
6   10   ?
5   15   8

The Gifts
of Great Minds

The figures next to the names of the 17 famous men pictured at right are taken from a study by a psychologist, Dr. Catherine Morris Cox, that estimates how they would score on a modern intelligence test. Many tabulations of test scores have shown that only 1 per cent of the population has an intelligence quotient, or I.Q., of more than 140. The estimated I.Q.s here average an amazing 166.

Throughout history, man seems to have produced a tiny handful of the highly endowed intellectually, whose forceful grasp of ideas has often opened new horizons for all men. Their extraordinary brains are probably products of environment as well as heredity; the mind develops prodigiously in the first three years of life, and recent studies show that lack of mental stimulation during this time actually impairs its growth. Given a stimulating environment, however, highly gifted minds seem to be irrepressible even in childhood, often begin exploring ideas at an astonishingly early age. Many of the gifted grow up to become artists, statesmen, scientists and philosophers, and a few influence others so profoundly with new ideas that they make history.

GALLERY OF GENIUSES
Dr. Cox's study of the intelligence of great men, including those shown here, examined those whose childhood days were well documented, and estimated their I.Q.s by their accomplishments. Mozart, for example, played three instruments at age six, Goethe wrote poetry at eight.

126

Drake 130   Grant 130   Washington

Lincoln 150   Napoleon 1

Rembrandt 155   Franklin 160

Galileo 185

Voltaire 190

Newton 190

Goethe 210

daVinci 180

Descartes 180

Kant 175

Mozart 165

Johnson 165

Luther 170

Jerome Snyder

6

Yardsticks
for Human
Intelligence

EVERYONE AGREES that intelligence is one of the most desirable of all human characteristics, but not everyone means the same thing when he talks about it. Intelligence refers, plainly, to an ability to perform mental operations successfully. But which operations are relevant? Memory certainly has something to do with intelligence; so does reasoning ability; so does inventiveness; so do a score of other mental capabilities. But what is the relative importance of all these capabilities? What of the individuals whose memory is good but whose inventiveness is poor? And what of those who are weak on abstract reasoning but who can build a complex cabinet, for example, after a cursory look at a blueprint? And to take the most extreme case, what of the "idiot savant"? This term refers to one who is well below par in performing many important mental operations but who has a few extraordinary capabilities.

One young man whose intelligence has been widely discussed in psychological literature was first brought to doctors for examination in 1937. "L" was then 11 years old, physically healthy, seemingly without neurological disturbances. His mental capabilities were rather oddly assorted:

• Given any date between the years of 1880 and 1950, he could name the day of the week.

• His powers of addition were formidable: he added the totals of 10 to 12 two-place numbers as fast as they were called out to him.

• He could spell many words forward or backward, with equal facility.

• He played by ear such compositions as Dvorak's "Largo"; could sing in toto the aria "Credo" and the duet "Si Pel Ciel" from the opera *Otello*.

But he did poorly in school. In general information he was vastly inferior to his classmates. Even if he could spell them backward, he knew the meanings of few words. Logical reasoning was almost totally beyond him, and he was lost in any question that involved abstraction.

Was "L" intelligent?

Half a century ago, the German psychologist William Stern said, "Intelligence is a general capacity of an individual consciously to adjust his thinking to new requirements: it is general mental adaptability to new problems and conditions." More recently, the American psychologist David Wechsler has said that intelligence is "the aggregate or global capacity of the individual to act purposefully, to think rationally and to deal effectively with his environment." Alfred Binet, the French psychologist, related it to "comprehension, invention, direction, and criticism"—or, summing these up, to "judgment."

This last view of intelligence may not be the most thoughtful ever proposed, but it will pay to consider it carefully, for Binet at least

AN INQUIRING INTELLIGENCE
Barry Wichmann of Rockwell City, Iowa, whose I.Q. of 162 puts him in the top 1 per cent of the nation, places a hair on a slide for examination under a microscope. Far from limiting his interests, his exceptional intelligence has boundless curiosity as a chief ingredient. Books, science, dramatics, history, world events, the conversation of adults all appeal to his active mind.

invested his own concept with a kind of objective meaning. He is the man who, early in this century, devised the first widely accepted intelligence test. It came about because he was appointed, in 1904, to a Government commission charged with the task of sorting out dull from normal students.

Mental versus chronological age

Binet found the proceedings of the commission frustrating in the extreme, principally because of the vagueness shrouding references to intellectual ability. Later, in an effort to clarify these concepts and find ways of measuring intellectual ability, he began to look into various mental tests then in existence. He also devised some of his own. In this project he was joined by Dr. Théodore Simon, a physician who had been working with backward children. From 1905 until 1911, when Binet died, the two men worked intensively at perfecting a reasonable test of intelligence. They tried tests of different abilities—of memory, for example, and of word-comprehension—on groups of children, searching for methods to distinguish the normal from the dull. Somewhere along the way, they hit upon the notion that certain levels of mental performance were usually reached at certain ages. From this they proceeded to the notion of a mental age as opposed to a chronological age. If an eight-year-old child could perform only as well as a normal six-year-old, he could be said to be two years retarded mentally. Thus the ultimate purpose of the original Binet-Simon test was to measure the number of years, if any, by which a child differed from the norm.

Soon after Binet died, however, Stern pointed to a rather obvious difficulty with this concept. The difficulty is that the significance of a two-year differential (let us say) is by no means the same at age four as it is at age 11. To get around this problem, Stern recommended relating the chronological age, not to the differential between the normal and subnormal but to the mental age itself, and thus "obtain[ing] the mental quotient." Stern's formula: "Mental quotient equals mental age over chronological age. An eight-year-old child with a mental age of six has . . . a mental quotient of six divided by eight equals .75."

Stern's "mental quotient" clearly foreshadows the later "intelligence quotient," or I.Q. The only real difference is that developers of the I.Q., in order to avoid the use of decimals, multiplied the quotient by 100. In Stern's own example, that would make the child's I.Q. 75; a child of normal ability, of course, has an I.Q. of 100. The inadequacies of Binet's concept of measuring intelligence—i.e., that children may be considered a given number of years ahead of or behind their age groups—become plain when the results of his method are compared to those obtained through the I.Q. method. At four years old, a child who is two

OEDIPUS AND THE SPHINX

In the centuries before intelligence tests, riddles were often used to measure superior shrewdness. This painting from a Fifth Century B.C. Greek cup depicts a sphinx asking Oedipus its famous riddle: what animal walks on four legs in the morning, two at noon, three in the evening? Oedipus' insight told him that a baby crawls, an adult walks upright, an old man uses a cane. For replying "man," he was made King of Thebes.

years in advance of his group has an I.Q. of 150 (six divided by four, multiplied by 100), and may well be a genius. But a child of eight who is two years ahead has an I.Q. of 125 (10 divided by eight, multiplied by 100)—which is above average but scarcely phenomenal. The Binet-Simon test was extensively improved in the United States, primarily because of the work of Professor Lewis M. Terman of Stanford University. Terman revised the Binet-Simon scales in 1916 and adapted them to American usage. At the same time, he established new intelligence norms on the basis of a sampling of some 1,000 American children and 400 adults. The Stanford-Binet test, as it came to be called, was widely popularized in the U.S. It was the first one in which the scoring was done on an I.Q. basis.

The change in telephones

The Stanford-Binet tests have been revised a number of times, and revisions will continue to be necessary from time to time simply because the everyday objects to which children are exposed, and about which they are questioned, are always changing. In the 1937 test, for example, three-year-old children were shown drawings of six objects and asked to name five of them. At the time the test was put together, 69 per cent of three-year-olds could do this. But by the 1950s, only 11 per cent of three-year-olds could. The trouble was that in the meantime several of the objects drawn—they included telephones and stoves—had undergone drastic changes in appearance.

Just what is it that these tests measure? In the Binet tradition, there is a heavy emphasis on abstract thinking and "judgment," but there is also some testing, especially at the lower ages, of accumulated information. For example, in the 1960 revision for two-year-olds a child is shown a picture of a doll and asked to point to parts of the body that are named. Three-year-olds, as suggested above, are asked to identify pictures of household objects. From six onward, the children are asked the meanings of words. However, their judgment is also tested, e.g., by asking them what they would do in certain everyday situations.

Simple memory tests begin at early ages and continue throughout the scale; at age 11, for example, children are asked to reproduce designs they have been shown and to repeat sentences that have been read to them. But by 11 the tests also push deeper into the child's abstract-reasoning capability: he is supposed to detect similarities among different groups of objects, to explain what is foolish or absurd in some sentences, and to analyze why people behave as they do in a story he is told. In the Average Adult test, abstract reasoning is weighted still more heavily. There are questions testing logical ability, the ability to reason arithmetically, to differentiate the meanings of words that are somehow related, to explain the thoughts underlying some proverbs, and so on.

The Stanford-Binet scales have been devised so that in any test of a sizable randomly distributed group, there will be a heavy "bunching" around the 100 mark; about 45 per cent of all those tested have I.Q.s of 90 to 110, which is considered normal. An I.Q. of over 130 puts one in the highest 3 per cent, of over 140 in the highest 1 per cent. An I.Q. of less than 80 puts one in the lowest 11 per cent. The "idiot savant" described at the beginning of this chapter, despite his several remarkable talents, had an I.Q. of only 50—which put him in the lowest 1 per cent.

Testing an ex-sergeant

Because the Stanford-Binet test was designed primarily for children, it is not very useful in testing adults. Dr. David Wechsler of Bellevue Psychiatric Hospital has devised a number of intelligence tests designed to make up for this deficiency. Part of the problem in using the Stanford-Binet on adults, Wechsler has observed, is simply that its content is too "babyfied," and this often made the psychologist's task difficult when he tried to establish rapport with his subject. He added, "Asking the ordinary housewife to furnish you with a rhyme to the words 'day,' 'cat' and 'mill,'" or an ex-Army sergeant to give you a sentence with the words 'boy,' 'river,' 'ball,' is not particularly apt to evoke either interest or respect."

The Wechsler Adult Intelligence Scale's own verbal tests are designed to minimize such problems, and much of the material consists of nonverbal "performance" tests—e.g., tests requiring the subject to make a meaningful sequence out of the drawings in a strip of cartoons, or to arrange blocks so that they re-create a given design. There is a high correlation between performances on the Stanford-Binet and the Wechsler (or WAIS), but it is not equally high for all kinds of subjects. Intellectually oriented persons tend to do relatively better on the Stanford-Binet than on the WAIS. On the other hand, those who score lowest on the Stanford-Binet tend to improve on the WAIS.

The varying scores achieved on these two tests, and on still others with different designs, may serve to emphasize an aspect of putting a yardstick to intelligence that is central, and yet often misunderstood: no test yet devised really can measure "raw intelligence," i.e., intelligence entirely divorced from the effects of experience. A higher-than-average performance may signify better-than-average experience as well as—or perhaps rather than—greater native ability. It is not that native ability is unimportant, but rather that it cannot be separated out in tests from the results of persistence, good study habits and an environment generally conducive to the development of intellectual skills. For this reason, a change in environment frequently portends a change in a child's score

I.Q. DISTRIBUTION CURVE

The bell-shaped curve at right demonstrates the statistical distribution of human intelligence as measured by intelligence quotient, or I.Q., tests: most people are concentrated within the range of 90 to 110 points of I.Q., while smaller numbers taper off toward the extremes of low and high intelligence. This particular curve reflects the scores of about 2,900 children on the Stanford-Binet test given by psychologist Lewis M. Terman. The distribution curve of intelligence is so well established that any test of a cross section of the population which resulted in a different curve would be quickly reevaluated and revised by its inventors.

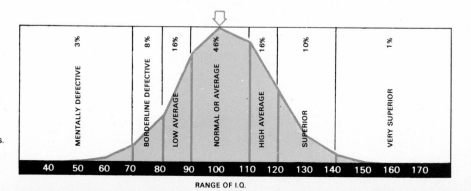

on an intelligence test. For any sizable group, it can be predicted with safety that scores in the future will be very close to scores in the past. But individual variations within the group may be considerable; sometimes they may involve improvements or deteriorations of as much as 50 points on an I.Q. scale. One study of repeatedly tested children has shown 59 per cent of them changing by 15 or more I.Q. points; 37 per cent changing by 20 or more points; and 9 per cent changing by 30 or more. To the extent that I.Q. tests measure intelligence, they indicate that intelligence can change during an individual's life.

This belief is fairly widely accepted nowadays, but not long ago most psychologists held the opposite, i.e., that intelligence was governed by heredity and, accordingly, invariable throughout life. A well-known 1934 textbook (*How the Mind Works*, by Burt, Miller, Moodie and Jones) put the argument strongly: "By intelligence, the psychologist understands inborn, all-around, intellectual ability. It is inherited, or at least innate, not due to teaching, or training. . . . Fortunately, it can be measured with accuracy and ease." Ironically, the accuracy and ease of measurement ultimately undermined beliefs in a fixed intelligence. As more and more individuals were tested, and greater confidence in the results established, it became impossible to ignore the evidence that intelligence could rise with education.

The discovery of this evidence ranks as a scientific event with profound social and political implications. For one thing, it lays to rest the age-old view that the human race is doomed to deterioration because the "wrong people"—e.g., the mentally inferior—have the most children.

And now that we know that any child's intelligence can be raised, there is greater interest in the question of how to raise that of the Negro and other groups that have consistently scored low on tests.

What might be done? The "ultimate solution," no doubt, is to rebuild the slum society that produces culturally impoverished children. But some psychologists and educators have concluded that the problem can be tackled without waiting for any such social transformation. They argue that some strenuous reforms in our lower schools are called for. They feel that the slum child is handicapped because he does not learn to read properly in the first two grades. To overcome this they propose that children start school at the age of three or four, instead of at five or six. In other words, make nursery school available to the slum child.

The malleable child

The importance of the nursery school is that it gets the child, at an age when he is still malleable, into a social setting where he is encouraged to think. Jean Piaget, the great Swiss psychologist who has devoted virtually his entire adult life to the study of children, has repeatedly emphasized the social nature of intellectual growth in young children. The so-called "pre-operational child"—age two to seven—is, in Piaget's view, intensely egocentric in his thinking and has no sense at all of objectivity in evaluating his own thoughts. He is apt to be totally unaware of large logical contradictions in his views. But if he is fortunate, he can be repeatedly forced to take note of the views of others, to test his own reasoning against the external realities thrust upon him in argument and discussion with others. It is this process that enables his intellectual powers to mature—and this would be part of a good nursery-school program. In Piaget's words, "The more a child has seen and heard, the more he wants to see and hear." The tragedy of the slum child is that he often never gets started on this spiral of intellectual growth.

History of a gifted group

The disabilities of the slum child may be put in sharper focus by a consideration of intellectually gifted children. By all odds, the most comprehensive—and fascinating—study of the gifted is one started more than four decades ago by Professor Terman, developer of the Stanford-Binet test and popularizer of the concept of the I.Q. Professor Terman conceived the idea of taking a group of gifted children and following their progress throughout life. The bulk of them had I.Q.s ranging from 135 to 200, with an average of 151.5 for the boys and 150.4 for the girls. Here is Professor Terman's description of the group: "All racial elements in the areas covered were represented in the group, including Orientals, Mexicans and Negroes. They came from all kinds of homes, from the poorest to the best, but the majority were the offspring of intellectually superior parents. . . . Nearly a third of the fathers as of 1922 were in professional occupations. . . . The number of books in the parents' homes, as estimated by the field assistants, ranged from almost none to 6,000, with one home out of six having 500 or more. . . ."

One point established early in the Terman study was that the intellectually gifted were apt to be physically and emotionally healthy, bearing no resemblance at all to the spindly, nearsighted, forlorn and bookish creatures who have populated so many stories about precocious children. Furthermore, the gifted children had fewer illnesses than children in a control group of average children set up for the purpose of comparison.

How did these extraordinarily promising children actually turn out in later life? Intelligence tests administered when their average age was 30 suffered from some technical shortcomings, but made it clear that the group was still in the highest 1 or 2 per cent. Other studies showed that 70 per cent of the men and 67 per cent of the women had graduated from college. More than 85 per cent of the men had "professional, managerial, official and semiprofessional" jobs.

In their personal lives, by 1955, when the average age was 44, 93.0 per cent of the men and 89.5 per cent of the women had married; of these, 20.7 per cent of the men and 22.1 per cent of the women had been divorced (both figures are slightly lower than the proportions for the general population). Their children were, not surprisingly, well above average intellectually, though they did not quite measure up to their gifted parents. Their I.Q.s, as measured on the Stanford-Binet scale, showed a concentration between 120 and 150.

The intelligence tests scored in terms of I.Q. do not measure all kinds of intellectual abilities. Indeed, there is still some dispute among psychologists whether they even measure the most important. Perhaps the most serious shortcoming of the I.Q. is that it tells us very little about an individual's creativity—i.e., about his potential as an original thinker or innovator.

Psychologists who have examined this domain closely, notably Jacob W. Getzels and Philip W. Jackson of the University of Chicago, are inclined to be critical of the accepted view of intelligence. Getzels and Jackson argued in *Creativity and Intelligence* that "the items on the typical intelligence test seemed to us to represent a rather narrow band of intellectual tasks. . . . To do well on the typical intelligence test, the subject must be able to recall and to recognize, perhaps even to solve; he need not necessarily be able to invent or innovate." It is these latter skills—those involved in what they call "the production of novelty" —that are involved in creativity.

Creativity versus I.Q.

To measure these creative skills, Getzels and Jackson devised several special tests. "What most of these tests had in common was that the score depended not on a single predetermined correct response as is most often the case with the common intelligence test, but on the number, novelty, and variety of adaptive responses to a given stimulus task." In an effort to find out the relationships, if any, between creativity and what might be called "I.Q. intelligence," Getzels and Jackson gave a number of adolescents both their own tests and several standard intelligence tests. Then they set up two groups: one was in the top 20 per cent in creativity but below that level on an I.Q. basis; the other was in the top 20 per cent on an I.Q. basis but below it in creativity. Some sense of the differences between the groups may be conveyed by two contrasting responses to one question in the creativity test. The subjects were shown a picture of a man lounging in a reclining seat on an airplane and asked to make up a story about him. The story produced by one high-I.Q. subject:

Mr. Smith is on his way home from a successful business trip.
He is very happy, and he is thinking about his wonderful family

DEFINITIONS OF GENIUS

- *"Genius . . . is the transcendent capacity for taking trouble first of all."*
  —THOMAS CARLYLE

- *"Genius does what it must, talent what it can."*
  —EDWARD ROBERT BULWER-LYTTON

- *"Art is a jealous mistress, and, if a man have a genius for painting, poetry, music, architecture, or philosophy, he makes a bad husband, and an ill-provider."*
  —RALPH WALDO EMERSON

- *"I have known no man of genius who had not to pay, in some affliction or defect either physical or spiritual, for what the gods had given him."*
  —MAX BEERBOHM

- *"A man of genius makes no mistakes. His errors are volitional and are the portals of discovery."*
  —JAMES JOYCE

- *"Every man of genius sees the world at a different angle from his fellows, and there is his tragedy."*
  —HAVELOCK ELLIS

- *"There is no great genius without some touch of madness."*
  —SENECA

and how glad he will be to see them again. He can picture it, about an hour from now, his plane landing at the airport and Mrs. Smith and their three children all there welcoming him home again.

One of the creative group came up with this:

This man is flying back from Reno where he has just won a divorce from his wife. He couldn't stand to live with her anymore, he told the judge, because she wore so much cold cream on her face at night that her head would skid across the pillow and hit him in the head. He is now contemplating a new skidproof face cream.

Getzels and Jackson found, as they had expected to, that there was only a low correlation between creativity and high I.Q.s. They were more interested in several other questions, however. One was: how well does the creative student do in his school work? The answer to this question was rather startling: despite the fact that the creative group's average I.Q. was 23 points lower than the other group's, the scholastic performances were about equal.

The Getzels-Jackson study makes it clear, then, that while intelligence tests are immensely useful, and will doubtless be with us a long time, we still do not know what these yardsticks actually measure.

Strange Landscapes from the Realm of Mental Illness

Freud once said that the artist creates a world of fantasies because his inner needs are "too clamorous" to be gratified in real life. The inner needs of the mentally ill are very clamorous indeed, and psychotics do indeed often turn to art. Inmates of mental institutions sometimes cover walls, floors and every scrap of paper with their drawings. Since Freud's time, physicians have learned to value this production, not only as a source of clues to their patients' problems, but also as a vivid, often harrowing picture of the psychotic mind itself. Most artists have the control to choose what they paint. The psychotic artist is at the mercy of his unconscious. He has no choice; he must illustrate the maelstrom which has him in its grip. As the pictures in this essay starkly show, psychotic art gives us a firsthand look at the unconscious itself—at the irrational fears, archaic symbols and private nightmares which lie buried deep in the minds of us all.

SIGNS OF MADNESS IN ART
This fragment, a depiction of hell by the early-16th Century artist Hieronymus Bosch, has been called "one of the most startling evocations of the diabolical known to painting." Not much is known about Bosch, but this scene has many features often associated with the art of psychotics: a crowded canvas, dismembered bodies, half-human monsters and gross anatomical distortions.

A Shattering Psychosis

One man's progressive withdrawal from reality to fantasy is clearly traced in the extraordinary series of cat paintings on these pages. They were done by an early-20th Century artist, Louis Wain. For some 20 years Wain painted sentimental and realistic cat portraits which captivated Londoners. He had immense popular success illustrating calendars, albums, postcards and the like. Most of his life he lived in seclusion with three spinster sisters and 17 cats. In his 57th year, indications of psychosis appeared both in his life and his art. He became convinced that enemies were influencing his mind with electrical impulses. At the same time, his cat portraits took an ominous turn.

Wain spent the last 15 years of his life in mental hospitals, a quaint and courtly figure who suffered recurring delusions of persecution. He drew and painted constantly—always cats. Indicative of his psychotic state are his cats' eyes, which stare with hostility even in an early drawing (left, below): the psychotic often feels that a threatening world is staring at him. Another indication is fragmentation of the body: images of the body undergo strange transformation in psychosis, and are almost never drawn without distortion. Wain's images eventually lost all coherence, but the baroque, infinitely detailed designs he produced were far more powerful and original than his former realism.

PROGRESSION OF PSYCHOSIS

The cat at the left above was painted during the early stages of Louis Wain's affliction. It differs from his earlier work not only in the alarming eyes but also in the spiked fur. Wain also replaced his usual landscape background with a formal design, an artistic defense against his sense of mental disorder. In the next portrait, the cat is quite hostile and a satanic red coloring predominates, particularly in the eyes—a projection of Wain's own fear that he was being victimized by evil spirits. The rainbow-colored halos around the cat are often found in psychotic art. In the late stages of schizophrenia, Wain's cats are almost abstract designs (above and opposite). Here realism completely disintegrated. Wain replaced it with obsessive, formal patterns in a desperate effort to organize and master his disordered thought processes.

Souish

SILENT SYMBOLISM

The crayon drawing below was made by a schizophrenic in his twenties, so withdrawn that he would not speak a word. The pigeons which make up the female figure, symbols for the breast, suggest that the youth was suffering from an abnormal attachment to his mother.

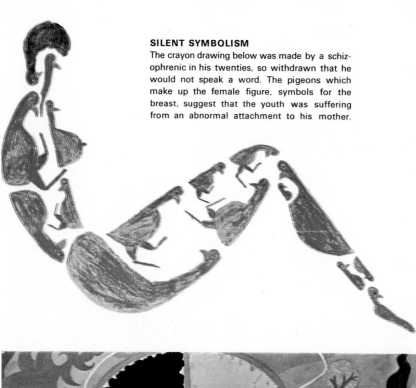

TERROR IN DISGUISE

Drawn by a Balkan peasant with delusions that witches, bears and white mice were threatening him, the vivid festival scene above at first seems to resemble simple folk art. The figure with a tail *(right)* is playing upon an "instrument" that is actually a small, distorted child.

PORTRAIT OF TORMENT

The Father (left) was painted by a guilt-ridden young girl, haunted by sexual yearnings for her father. On the calm right side her torment is repressed, but on the left side roosters and suns (both father symbols) appear among the sinister arabesques that pour out of the head.

140

The Imagery of Schizophrenia

The art of schizophrenics is extremely varied in form, for there are many different forms that schizophrenia can take, from morbid apathy to violent outbursts and bizarre hallucinations. In essence, the schizophrenic mind draws in upon itself, substituting private fantasies for a harsh and threatening real world. But the unconscious overwhelms the psychotic's vulnerable world; he lives in a waking nightmare of images, symbols and disordered thoughts which tumble out in his art. When the schizophrenic paints, he attempts to portray the strange demons that haunt his mind. His repressed ideas are brought forth in the form of obscure symbols. He uses vivid, contrasting colors to portray his intense emotions, and may try to paint sounds. He may even cover a finished canvas with titles, afraid that he has failed to convey his turbulent fantasies. In each respect this art reflects illness, although the results can be exquisite. For example, distortion of the human figure, reflecting the patient's disrupted human relations, can give paintings the look of enchanting primitive art.

Symbols inside a Skull

The grotesque painting at left, reminiscent of Hieronymus Bosch's art, was made by a 26-year-old schizophrenic artist. Raised on a prairie farm in midwestern Canada, he had experienced such a brutal childhood that he had become extremely withdrawn, eventually retiring into a private world of weird fantasies. In one of these, he imagined that if he cut the flesh off his arm (lower right chamber) he would be shocked back into human feelings. When he actually made some cuts on his arm, he was admitted to a hospital for psychiatric treatment. Here he set to work on the painting he called *The Maze*.

He had great difficulty talking to people. Yet when he began to paint, the images of his torment poured out with remarkable clarity. He portrayed himself lying in an open field, his skull cut open to reveal the painful memories of his past and the morbid fantasies of his present state. Once the imagery of his illness emerged, the artist could step back from the canvas and talk to his doctor about his torment. In time he recovered and married. He still paints, although with a less morbid outlook.

SCHIZOPHRENIC SELF-PORTRAIT
In the strange self-portrait at left, the artist's open skull is divided like the maze a psychologist uses to observe a rat's behavior. In the central compartment lies the rat, the artist himself, exhausted in defeat after entering each chamber. The various chambers depict bitter incidents in the artist's childhood, his disillusion (the "Museum of Hopelessness"), and his cynicism (dancers seen as puppets). His doctors are seen in one chamber as crows tormenting a helpless lizard while in an adjoining chamber they scrutinize the artist in a test tube.

Moods
of Madness

Some psychoses take the form of abnormal extremes of mood, most often depression and mania. In these disorders, compared to schizophrenia, the psychotic's contact with reality may be relatively unimpaired; he knows it is he and not the world around him which has changed. He is so engulfed by his uncontrollable mood, however, that he can paint nothing else; like the schizophrenic artist, his subject is his psychosis.

The depressive may show little interest in art, although he may paint more easily than he can talk. When he does paint, he bears witness to the depths of his hopeless despair. His figures are in postures of terrible self-rejection and shame *(right)*, his colors are somber, often black alone or black with dark red. In extreme cases, he may see himself as dead.

The manic, in contrast, lives in a state of hyperexcitement. He paints in swirls and agitated lines, releasing excess physical energy. Outlines are usually bold, colors hot and contrasting. Yet the manic's excitement is a mask for the same feelings of failure and frustration felt by the depressive. His thin veneer of gaiety may explode, and underneath a furious guilt and anger are revealed. For both depressive and manic, art can be therapeutic. It requires no anxiety-producing therapist present, no struggle with words as does an interview. Alone, he can find relief by drawing his moods outside of himself and putting them down on paper.

AN UNCONTROLLABLE FURY
This is a graphic picture of what it feels like to be seized by a raging mood. The young patient who painted it told her doctor that the red network emanating from her brain was sparks. Her clenched fists and ferocious teeth indicate her hatred both of herself and her seizures.

PORTRAIT OF DESPAIR
In the self-portrait at right, a middle-aged depressive shows herself in a forlorn, kneeling posture, surrounded by a deep red background which represents her imagined sins. In talking about the picture she told her doctor, "I am an evil woman: black surrounded by scarlet."

1885

1887

1888

Van Gogh and the "Rage of Work"

Following an attack of "unbearable hallucinations," the great Dutch painter Vincent Van Gogh wrote his brother, "Let me go quietly on with my work; if it is that of a madman, well, so much the worse." Van Gogh started to draw at the age of 27. Before he ended his life a decade later, he lived in urban garrets, in barren rooms of rural cottages and in the wards of mental institutions. His moods shifted from profound discouragement to the highest pitch of enthusiasm, from what he called the "rage of work" to the "fear and horror of madness." He went insane for days and even weeks at a time. Yet he captured the suffering of mental illness in glittering, agitated canvases and, in the intervals between the worst attacks, he painted some of his most lyric and peaceful scenes.

From his paintings, his letters and his life, it is apparent that Van Gogh suffered from some psychosis whose nature is unclear. In the midst of a quarrel, he once hurled a glass of absinthe at his friend, the French painter Paul Gauguin. Gauguin took the distraught artist home and put him to bed. The next night Van Gogh came at Gauguin with a razor, then abruptly fled back to his room, where he cut off a part of his ear *(above, opposite)* in an excess of guilt. In the last letter to his brother, found on Van Gogh at the time of his death, he wrote, "Well, my own work, I am risking my life for it and my reason has half foundered because of it."

COMPASSION AND PEACE
After severing his ear, Van Gogh was taken to the hospital at Arles where he suffered delirium and hallucinations for three days. In the calmer aftermath of his illness, he painted the hospital ward *(right)* as a subdued and tranquil scene, his peaceful figures seen with compassion.

PORTRAITS OF THE ARTIST

The series of self-portraits at left shows the radical change of style in Van Gogh's work as the artist struggled against the threat of his growing madness. Departing from the soft Impressionism of the 1887 portrait, he turned to stiff brush strokes and odd, broken swirls of color.

LAST SELF-PORTRAIT

Painted two months before his death, the last self-portrait *(above)* is one of Van Gogh's greatest masterpieces. In the swirling background and the wavy tension of the head, it reflects both the sadness and terror within the man, and the final firmness of a great artist's hand.

Van Gogh's End

Throughout his later years, Vincent Van Gogh painted to preserve himself from utter madness. "The work distracts my mind," he wrote, "and I *must* have some distraction." Indeed the remarkable power of his art lies in the tension between artistic control and the underlying sense of chaos. In his last paintings, elements of psychosis and artistic genius merged: Van Gogh's unique style incorporated exaggerations characteristic of psy-chotic art, yet this gave his work a message all men could grasp. Few psychotic artists have been able to do this. The Spanish artist Francisco Goya, for example, covered the walls of his home with witches, vampires and ghosts during his psychotic episodes, writing that "the sleep of reason begets monsters." In the end, Van Gogh preferred death to the sleep of reason, shooting himself after painting the wheatfield below.

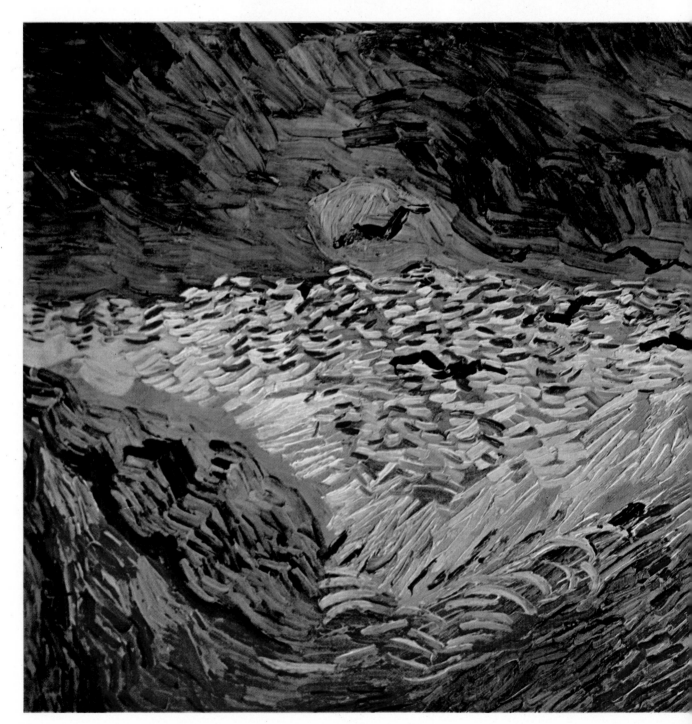

"CORNFIELD WITH LARK," 1887
The spring cornfield at left, painted in one of Van Gogh's calmer periods, reflects his abiding love of nature. The lone lark gliding over the green corn embodies the renewal of life.

"WHEATFIELD WITH CROWS," 1890
Van Gogh shot himself in the wheatfield where he painted his last canvas *(below)*. The fateful crows rise up as the "road of life" abruptly ends in the midst of the wild yellow wheat.

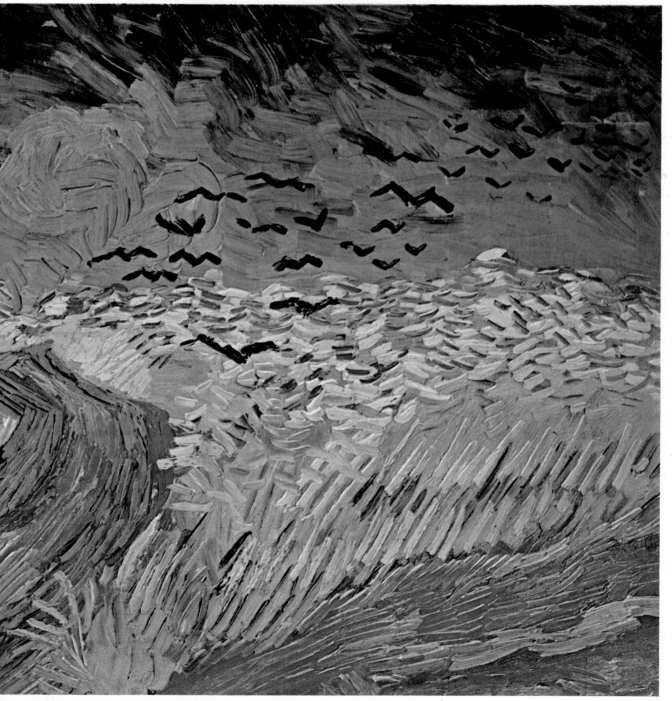

149

"Black Angels . . . at My Cradle"

"Disease and insanity were the black angels on guard at my cradle," wrote the Norwegian artist Edvard Munch, the first of the modern Expressionist painters. At the age of five Munch watched his mother, ill with tuberculosis, die of a hemorrhage. Thereafter he was raised by a strict and threatening father. "When he punished us," Munch recalled, "he could become almost insane in his violence." Until he was 45, Munch struggled to overcome incipient psychosis by painting the images of his tortured past. A distinctive, schizophrenic trait of his art was the use of straight or wavy parallel lines around a central, often distorted figure. These lines expressed his fear of being engulfed in a hostile world. In his woodcuts, Munch used the natural grain of the wood for this effect—a lasting technical innovation in the printmaker's art.

From his 45th year on, Munch was almost continuously psychotic. During the rest of his life, the artist in effect replaced the real world with the world of his own paintings. He became a recluse, surrounded himself with his canvases and would rarely part with one. He said his pictures were too jealous to be exhibited with the works of other artists. He called his creations his children, and when dissatisfied with a painting, he would occasionally beat it with a whip. Echoing his own father, he said this "horse treatment" improved its character.

FATHER AND SON

In the painting above, entitled *Jealousy,* Munch places a sallow lover between a red-faced father-figure and a woman with seductive hair. Munch, who often painted women's hair entwining men's necks, had a stormy love life, considered women vampires. Of a friend who had recently married he said, "After a few months he was only soup . . . ashen and empty-eyed."

THE CRY OF THE UNCONSCIOUS

With *The Cry (opposite),* a picture of pure terror, Munch launched the school of Expressionism. He painted it after watching a sunset in which the clouds, to him, resembled "coagulated blood." He was painting—unconsciously —an image of his mother's fatal hemorrhage.

7

Manipulations of Mentality

THE USE OF DRUGS AND ALCOHOL predates history. These were the original "mood changers," long before this term was coined to characterize the tranquilizers and antidepressants that have entered and enriched the 20th Century pharmacopoeia. Alcohol and drugs like opium were used to forget the cares of the world—if only temporarily. They were used in medicine because of their physical effect in reducing or eliminating pain. Until nitrous oxide and chloroform came into use, during the first half of the 19th Century, alcohol was commonly used as an anesthetic in surgical procedures. Until the recent synthesis of such new narcotics as methadone, opium was routinely prescribed as a pain-killer. Alcohol achieves its pain-killing effect by slowing down, or "depressing," the central nervous system, with the result that all the body's responses are dulled. First consciousness is clouded; then, if enough alcohol is taken, it is blocked out altogether. The first centers to be affected are those of the cortex, the centers that control the highest and most civilized aspects of mental functioning and behavior. This explains why critical judgment is impaired and inhibitions are released, with the result that the individual is likely to do and say things he would not do and say under normal circumstances. The retiring man may become rambunctious, the gentle one aggressive.

Opium and its derivatives, morphine and codeine, also act as depressants but achieve their results in a more complicated way. Morphine and codeine, incidentally, are still prescribed for pain. The danger in the use of these narcotic drugs does not lie in their initial effects or in their tendency to produce euphoria. The trouble is that virtually anyone who takes a drug like morphine or heroin over even a short period of time becomes addicted to it. The body habituates itself to the drug's effects, with the result that larger and larger doses are required to produce the same changes in mood.

Moreover, habituation seems to involve actual changes in the functioning of the entire body. The user continues to obtain release from tension and anxiety, but as his body builds up a tolerance for the drug, he needs more and more of it. Morphine addicts have been known to take, as a matter of routine, doses which would immediately be lethal to a normal person. The addict becomes physically and psychologically dependent on the drugs so that in the end he continues to take the drugs simply to avoid the horrors that giving it up—withdrawal—would involve.

Alcohol, too, can produce habituation and even addiction, although these physical effects and the tendency of anyone to succumb to them seem to be only part of the story in the disorder known as alcoholism. Studies have shown that in some cases there does seem to be a relationship between an individual's biochemistry and his reaction to alcohol.

MAGIC MUSHROOMS
An Indian priestess in a remote part of southern Mexico prepares mushrooms of a kind her tribe has called "divine" for centuries because they produce ecstatic visions. Eating these is a sacred ceremony, followed by a night spent praying and experiencing hallucinations. The power of drugs like this one to transform the workings of the mind has awed man from his beginnings.

HENBANE

OPIUM

HEMP

Social and economic factors also appear to play a part in the development of alcoholism. In some ethnic groups and nations alcoholism is far less common than it is in others, so it appears that a tendency to become an alcoholic has some connection with the social attitude toward wine and liquor. And it is becoming increasingly well established that individual personality factors play a major role in the development of alcoholism, even though there seems to be no single personality type for the alcoholic.

Neurotic cats and alcohol

Current psychiatric opinion is that alcoholism is less a disease than a symptom that is common to a variety of psychiatric illnesses, and that alcohol may provide a convenient relief for the discomforts they bring. Laboratory experiments have shown, for example, that cats which have been driven to neurosis—by exposure to various situations that create conflict—are more willing to drink alcohol when it is presented to them than normal cats are. Under the influence of alcohol, the neurotic animals are less likely than others to display fear.

Not all of the traditional chemical mood-changers function as depressants. Cocaine, for example, stimulates the central nervous system and produces excitement, a feeling of self-confidence and great strength. For centuries, the natives of Bolivia and Peru have been cheering themselves up by chewing the leaves of the coca shrub, the active ingredient of which is cocaine. But cocaine, too, is addictive. Its modern counterparts, benzedrine and the other drugs of the amphetamine group, are less dangerous, but they, too, can lead to acute intoxication, even hallucinations and delusions.

Increasing interest in the mind and in the problem of mental illness has brought about in recent years a tremendous spurt in the development of other kinds of mood-changing drugs, the best known of which are the tranquilizers and antidepressants. When the tranquilizers and antidepressants were first introduced, they were viewed virtually as panaceas for mental illness. But many did not live up to expectations. Many show evidence of having addictive qualities and of producing undesirable physical side effects. In addition, they do no more for severe mental cases than their names imply: they tranquilize and they reduce depression, they diminish agitation and lessen apathy. But agitation and apathy are symptoms rather than diseases in themselves. Tranquilizers and antidepressants may make a mental patient accessible to psychotherapy. They may enable him to function satisfactorily in a supervised environment, but they do not, of themselves, constitute cures.

The "original" tranquilizer discovered by man was rauwolfia, a plant long used in India in the treatment of a variety of illnesses. Reserpine,

SEDUCTIVE PLANTS
The leaves and seeds of certain plants have been a source of drugs for centuries. Dried or ground, smoked or chewed, they have various effects. Those at left are among the most familiar. Henbane produces hallucinations. Opium leads to euphoria, sometimes ending in sleep. Hemp (or hashish) smokers may be unable to talk coherently or control spasms of giggling.

an extract of rauwolfia, was first used in the West to reduce high blood pressure. (The tranquilizers now available are of many different chemical compositions.) The antidepressants—again, of many different chemical compositions—were discovered by accident in 1952 when an experimental drug called Iproniazid was synthesized and used in the treatment of tuberculosis. It seemed to be effective in attacking the bacteria that cause tuberculosis but it had one side effect that was extremely undesirable in tubercular patients. Tuberculars need rest, but Iproniazid elevated their mood and encouraged them to be active.

Eloquent records of fantasies

Tranquilizers and antidepressants have a limited aim: to bring the user into a more tolerable relationship with himself and his environment. But drugs exist that produce what might be called transcendent experiences: dramatic alterations of consciousness and perception, which can be experienced literally as revelation. Many of these hallucinogens have long been associated with primitive religions and religious rites. Central American Indians built cults around the experiences that came to them in consequence of chewing mescaline, a product of the peyote cactus. Belladonna, thorn apple and henbane, common European plants that are also hallucinogens, appear to have been among the standard ingredients of the medieval witches' brew. Hemp, or marijuana, has a history of use for mystical purposes which stretches back thousands of years. Psilocybin is used by Mexican Indians; they get it in mushrooms they call the Sacred Fungus, or "divine mushrooms."

People who have taken various hallucinogens experimentally have eloquently recorded the results:

Banker R. Gordon Wasson, after eating the "divine mushrooms," had visions "in vivid color, always harmonious . . . palaces all laid over with semiprecious stones . . . a mythological beast drawing a regal chariot. Later it was as though the walls of our house had dissolved, and my spirits had flown forth, and I was suspended in mid-air viewing landscapes of mountains, with camel caravans advancing slowly across the slopes, the mountains rising tier above tier to the very heavens. . . ."

Psychologist Havelock Ellis, after taking mescaline, saw "thick, glorious fields of jewels" that "would spring up into flower-like shapes beneath my gaze, and then seem to turn into gorgeous butterfly forms." With the same drug novelist Aldous Huxley saw in a small vase of flowers "what Adam had seen on the morning of his creation—the miracle . . . of naked existence . . . the divine source of all existence . . . words like 'grace' and 'transfiguration' came to my mind."

The drug that has been most widely experimented with in recent years —and the subject of the most violent debate—is lysergic acid diethyla-

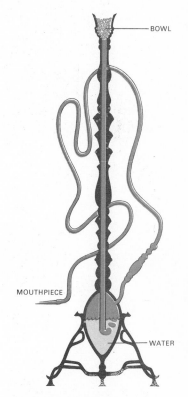

BOWL

MOUTHPIECE

WATER

SMOKING TROUBLES AWAY
Hashish, the Arabic name for a hemp plant, is sometimes smoked in a hookah, or water pipe, in the Middle East. The leaves are burned in the bowl at top, the smoke drawn through water. The drug goes under a variety of names in different countries—bhang, charas, kif, marijuana and pot—and is often smoked in cigarettes, known in the U.S. as reefers.

mide (LSD). Like the other hallucinogens, LSD is derived from a natural product, ergot, a fungus that grows on rye and that was used originally in medicine for the treatment of excessive bleeding and migraine headaches. The discovery of LSD was another one of the accidents in which scientific history abounds. It came about in 1943, when the Swiss chemist Dr. Albert Hofmann, who was experimenting with an ergot compound called lysergic acid, added some new molecules to it and somehow or other absorbed some of the resulting mixture into his system, perhaps through the pores of his skin. Shortly thereafter he found himself unable to go on working.

"I had to go home," Hofmann wrote in his laboratory report, "because I experienced a very peculiar restlessness which was associated with a slight attack of dizziness. I went to bed and got into a not unpleasant state of drunkenness which was characterized by an extremely stimulating fantasy. When I closed my eyes . . . I experienced fantastic images of an extraordinary plasticity. They were associated with an intense kaleidoscopic play of colors."

"I saw my body . . . dead"

A second and somewhat larger dose, which he took when he realized that his chemical must have been responsible for his experience, had even more startling results. "I lost all control of time; space and time became more and more disorganized and I was overcome with fears that I was going crazy. The worst part of it was that I was clearly aware of my condition though I was incapable of stopping it. Occasionally I felt as being outside my body. I thought I had died. My 'ego' was suspended somewhere in space and I saw my body lying dead on the sofa. I observed and registered clearly that my 'alter ego' was moving around the room, moaning."

This effect was produced by only 250 micrograms—a mere speck—of the chemical.

The experiences reported by experimenters with LSD since Hofmann vary widely, from the horrifying to the transcendent. Subjects report rapid flights of ideas and associations over which they have little control; they may answer questions irrelevantly and utter trivialities as profundities. They may become silent and withdrawn, utterly fascinated by their fantasies and images. The visual experiences associated with LSD seem extremely difficult to describe; many subjects have reported, for example, that they "hear" sound as color, as ribbon or tape drifting across a room.

Since LSD was discovered, close to 1,000 research papers have been published on it and scores of thousands of individual experiences with LSD recorded. But as Dr. James M. Dille of the University of Washington has said, "Investigation in this area is difficult. Those of us who have worked with LSD and human subjects know the diversity of reactions it produces. In some, the LSD experience is filled with reward and gratification. In others there is terror and indescribable fear. This diversity of effect is quite confusing. Yet it is this very diversity of effect which presents the challenge to investigators. . . ."

Here is a summary of what has been learned, derived from many well-qualified sources but particularly from the work of Dr. Sidney Cohen of the University of California School of Medicine, a preeminent authority in the field.

The three main hallucinogens—LSD, psilocybin and mescaline—differ only in the amount of the drug needed to achieve its effect and its duration. The effects of LSD and mescaline usually last eight to 10 hours; psilocybin works for four to five hours. LSD is 100 times as powerful as psilocybin, 7,000 times as powerful as mescaline.

LSD and "mental set"

From the data on "almost 5,000 individuals who had received either LSD or mescaline during more than 25,000 occasions," Dr. Cohen concluded that with proper precautions "they are safe when given to a selected healthy group"—i.e., people who are not seriously sick either physically or mentally. (Psilocybin was not included in this survey.)

The hallucinogens can provide a rewarding, esthetic, philosophical or religious experience. Some people, for example, have had an abrupt sense of comprehending the nature of God. However, the effect of the drug depends a great deal on the "mental set" of the user and the environment in which it is taken. If taken in expectation of a rewarding experience and in a pleasant setting, in the company of someone who is an expert on these drugs, the experience will probably be pleasant.

For a while, as little as 15 minutes or as long as two hours after a dose of LSD is taken, nothing happens. As the drug takes effect, the physical symptoms may include muscular tension, tingling, trembling, a rapid pulse, deep respiration, localized pain. But ordinarily there are only slight feelings of chilliness and perhaps an enlargement of the pupils of the eyes. Nausea or headache seldom occurs.

The earliest and most common manifestation of LSD is a tremendous intensification of visual perception—in Dr. Cohen's words, "as though a translucent membrane has been peeled from one's eyes for the first time." Everything becomes clearer, brighter, sharper, with different dimensions and qualities. The subject may spend hours rapt in contemplation of a piece of wood or a stone, feeling that he is comprehending at last the essential nature of these things.

Later may come active illusions. As Dr. Hofmann noted of his original

DISTORTED BY LSD
This sketch, reprinted from a Swiss scientific journal, was drawn by a subject under the influence of lysergic acid diethylamide (LSD), and illustrates how his body seemed to him at the time. Other subjects have reported that hands and feet sometimes feel abnormally long or short, heavy or light, or disconnected from the body.

LSD experience, these come and go with "extraordinary plasticity": there are crystalline landscapes, jewel-encrusted mountains of gold, geometric patterns, flowers, birds, butterflies, fountains of color. These may give way to actual scenes, animals, objects, people, voices from early childhood—and the subject may "relive" experiences from the past. Another common effect has been called "humanity identification." This is "fantasies in which the patient feels love, grief, loneliness or physical suffering as though he is experiencing them as they have been felt by all people at all times and places." All this while, however, even if under intense emotional distress, the subject can observe his own situation—he knows where he is and what he is doing.

After several hours the effect of the drug gradually begins to fade. Usually within eight hours the subject's condition returns to normal, although for several days or even weeks afterward feelings of well-being, depression or anxiety occasionally recur.

LSD and schizophrenia

When work was first begun with LSD, considerable hope was held out that it could be used as an aid in understanding the nature of schizophrenia: volunteers who took it in experiments sometimes displayed many of the symptoms and signs of this most dreaded mental illness. Nothing definite has been discovered in this connection. There was also hope that it could be used in the treatment of alcoholism and the neuroses. Here too, nothing definite has been established but investigation continues. As yet, there is no evidence that it is addictive. But experimentation is still too new for this fact to be verified. All that is known with certainty is that in the hands of careful experimenters these drugs may in time help unlock many of the secrets of the human mind and its functioning.

Many kinds of chemical mood-changers can now be produced, including drugs with marked selective action. The tranquilizers, for example, calm, but they do not make people drowsy or put them to sleep as do the barbiturates. Euphoriants incapacitate their users by making them idiotically cheerful. There are drugs in gas form that can produce terror: given one whiff under experimental conditions, cats shy away from mice in abject fear. There are depressants that sink their victims into unspeakable pessimism. All these drugs are still in a highly experimental state, but there seems to be no question that they will one day be perfected for widespread use in medicine to help control mental illness by manipulating the mind.

The form of mental manipulation familiar to most people is probably hypnosis, which, as noted earlier in this book, was used by pioneer neurologists, including Freud, in the treatment of hysteria. (The origin and present-day uses of hypnosis in psychiatry are illustrated and discussed in the picture essay following this chapter.)

From its formal introduction in the 18th Century, hypnosis has been the subject of argument on ethical grounds: most people find the idea that one person can be made completely subject to the will of another intrinsically alarming. But hypnosis requires a relationship of trust between the hypnotist and his subject; it is improbable that anyone can be hypnotized against his will. And even a subject in a deep hypnotic trance is not likely to be persuaded to violate his own moral code, for although hypnosis can bring certain behavior patterns to the surface, it cannot create new patterns that are foreign to the subject's personality.

More drastic effects on the mind can be produced by a technique which has come to be called "brainwashing" by those opposed to its use, or "thought reform" or "control" by those employing it. This technique is in essence an attempt to change a person's attitudes; to force him to take up beliefs that may be diametrically opposed to the ones he originally held; to change his political or moral position; to commit treason.

Brainwashing employs three phases: (1) the victim is disoriented and disillusioned; (2) he is interrogated; (3) his disorientation is exploited. The first stage aims to build up a feeling of complete psychological isolation in the victim. He is deprived of regular meals and sleep, of companionship and reading matter. The rhythm of his life is deliberately disrupted. After some weeks of this, he becomes depressed; he begins to lose his sense of personal identity. He is then ready for interrogation. Often he welcomes this as a form of human contact and a pleasant variation to the demoralizing life he has been leading.

The torment of brainwashing

But the interrogation is far from an easy experience. By now the victim cannot concentrate on details. He becomes confused about the validity of his own experience. He is extremely amenable to suggestion. The interrogator takes advantage of this sense of disorientation by twisting and distorting the victim's words. He changes parts of his victim's statements and then presents these alterations as authentic parts of the originals. Apparently caught in contradictions, the victim begins to wonder about his own memory. The interrogations occur at unexpected hours of the day and night, and continue for unpredictable lengths of time. The purpose is to produce maximum confusion and anxiety, so that eventually the victim finds it virtually impossible to distinguish truth from falsehood. By this time he is likely to be prepared to do or say anything to gain release from his mental torment. A "confession" is presented to him and, in all probability, he will sign it.

Now the last stage—the stage of conversion—is initiated. The victim

HYPNOSIS IN FICTION

In his 1894 novel *Trilby*, from which this picture is taken, George du Maurier tells of a beautiful, tone-deaf girl who is hypnotized into submission and a brilliant singing career by the evil Svengali. The story ends with Svengali's death and Trilby's return to anonymity. *Trilby* endows hypnotism with fictitious powers. In fact, hypnotism cannot make a poor voice beautiful or give a hypnotist total rule over his subject.

is treated kindly, almost as a convalescent. His living conditions are improved. His instructors tell him in detail what he must think, not only about the present and the future, but also about the past. Knowing that any kind of decent life for him now depends on his compliance, the victim complies.

While it is tempting to blame modern psychology for the development of this extreme technique of persuasion, it is more likely that it was developed through trial and error. And the technique appears to have only a temporary effect, particularly if its victims are subsequently moved into milieus which do not approve of their new views. Captured American soldiers who were brainwashed by the Chinese Communists during the Korean War and subsequently returned to the West were found after a while to have returned to their original ways of thinking as well. After a time they regarded the whole episode as a terrifying and traumatic, but essentially transient, experience.

The origins of all our beliefs lie in the environment in which we are born and grow up, in the attitudes of our parents, in the things we are taught at school, in the social and economic group we belong to. The educational process which creates a feeling of security and personal worth provides a built-in resistance to attempts to manipulate the mind against the will of its possessor.

Hypnosis, Drugs and "Thought Control"

The picture on the opposite page shows the beginning of an experiment in which one man (right) takes another back through the years and causes him to behave as though he were a child again. How the experiment came out is shown in pictures on pages 164 and 165. The powerful force behind it is hypnosis—one of several techniques man has developed for manipulating behavior drastically. Most of them have been known for centuries, although they have come to be better understood in recent years. Hypnosis, for example, first caused a public sensation nearly 200 years ago. Drugs—a widely used means of changing mood and behavior since ancient times—are now the subject of intensive medical research. New ones are being discovered. Changing men's allegiance by persuasion is nothing new either, but in modern times such practices as brainwashing and mass propaganda have been refined to the point of extraordinary effectiveness.

THE BEGINNING: A TOUCH
Psychiatrist Herbert Spiegel touches the face of Jim, a volunteer who has been hypnotically prepared for this signal in a previous session and goes immediately into a hypnotic state. Dr. Spiegel, associated with Columbia University's College of Physicians and Surgeons, is using hypnosis as a scientific research tool to investigate the development of personality at various age-levels.

Mesmer and the Power of Suggestion

In the picture on page 161 a contemporary psychiatrist is employing the technique of hypnosis, first used medically by an Austrian doctor named Franz Anton Mesmer, who arrived in Paris in 1778 with a strange cure for many illnesses. He would wave his hands over his patients, or touch them, or even touch inanimate objects which they then touched—and they would go into fits or trances. Afterward they often felt better. Mesmer called his force "animal magnetism," and believed it to be an invisible fluid which flowed from him to other persons or things. Mesmerism, as this treatment came to be called, became an instant sensation in Paris. Thousands of sufferers flocked to his salon. Crowds became so uncontrollable that Mesmer once "magnetized" a tree so thousands could be treated by clinging to ropes tied to the tree.

Mesmer's success was short-lived. A French Royal Commission investigated mesmerism, and in 1785 pronounced it dangerous. Discredited, his cure an object of ridicule (opposite), Mesmer left Paris for good.

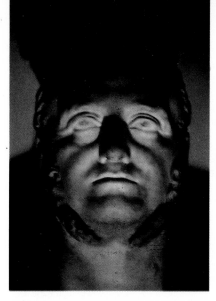

MISSIONARY MESMERIST
The dramatically lighted bust shown above is of John Elliotson, a 19th Century English doctor who devoted himself to popularizing mesmerism, but failed to make it medically respectable.

MESMERISM MOCKED
The cartoon on the opposite page, published in Paris in the 1780s, pictured a mesmerist as an ass. Titled *The Magic Finger, or Animal Magnetism*, it shows Mesmer's method of inducing trances with passes of his hands. At top, two female patients are depicted as silly sheep.

"ANIMAL MAGNETISM" AT WORK
This contemporary drawing shows a feature of Mesmer's Paris salon: the *baquet*, a round tub in which were placed bottles of "magnetized" water. Some patients treated their maladies by touching afflicted areas with rods and ropes connected to the tub; others, like the woman in the chair at right, were put in trance. Another *baquet* is visible through the door.

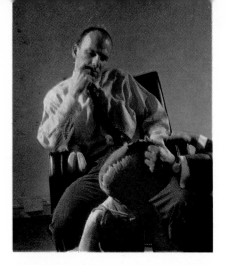

A 10-YEAR-OLD'S DISTRESS

Dr. Spiegel's hypnotized subject, Jim *(above)* has just been told it is his tenth birthday. He stares at a large stuffed doll offered as a present, which he thinks much too babyish for him.

The Many Ages of Jim

How or why hypnosis works is largely conjectural, but it is essentially the art of putting a subject into an extremely responsive state. It is widely and beneficially used in medicine, psychiatry and psychological research.

The human nervous system records sensations, directs voluntary activity, remembers and thinks—and all these functions are to some degree put at the disposal of the hypnotist by a subject in a hypnotized state. Thus, in medicine, a hypnotized patient can be disassociated from the sensation of pain. In psychiatry, he can be directed to recall significant memories. The pictures on these pages show hypnosis being used by a psychiatrist to learn more about the effects of early life experience on personality. (The beginning of this experiment is pictured on page 161.) The subject is in effect returned to the state of his development at childhood age-levels.

A FOUR-YEAR-OLD'S DELIGHT

At another spoken signal from Dr. Spiegel, Jim, still hypnotized, now thinks he is four. After the signal was given, his attitude toward the doll immediately changed, and he became delighted with it. Here Dr. Spiegel has just tried to take it away. Jim protests, "You said I could have it."

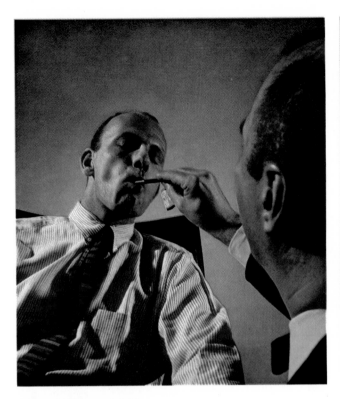

FROM INFANCY TO TWO

The pictures on this page show Jim's behavior with a felt pen at four different age-levels. Above left: Jim believes himself to be one month old as Dr. Spiegel hands him the closed pen. He sucks on it with eyes closed. Above right: after being told that he is two years old, he holds the pen in a childlike grip and scribbles aimlessly. His hand coordination and scribbles were just the same as those of genuine two-year-olds.

FROM FOUR TO 10

Believing himself four *(above),* clutching a rabbit he called "bunny," Jim draws a crude man. At right, a mature 10, he draws an Indian and signs his name. According to one theory, hypnotized subjects unconsciously act out roles merely to please the hypnotist, but Dr. Spiegel has found that his subjects are relatively poor imitators of children both when unhypnotized and when hypnotized without being regressed.

The Potent Effects of Drugs

Man can alter the way his mind works by a means far less dramatic than hypnosis: by injecting small amounts of certain drugs into the bloodstream that bathes his brain. His strange willingness to surrender control of his mental life is indicated by his historic voluntary use of drugs. He has long used mild ones for pleasure (below), and strong ones such as alcohol, opium and heroin to such excess that they pose grave social problems.

In the 1940s, man began to synthesize drugs which turned out eventually to produce various effects on the nervous system. One of the most startling of these man-made drugs is LSD (lysergic acid diethylamide), which seems to inhibit the brain centers that integrate perception. A tiny amount causes a loss of coherent identity similar to schizophrenia, and produces overwhelmingly vivid but disconnected sensations and visions (opposite).

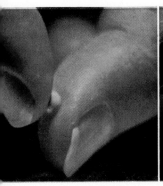

AN LSD EXPERIENCE

The sequence above is from a film of an LSD experiment. A woman takes the drug in pill form and lies down, wearing an eyeshade to exclude outside impressions and heighten those originating from within. At right above, with eyeshade removed, her face reflects the intensity of a vision in which she sees herself simultaneously outside and inside a brightly colored cave.

VISIONS FROM A ROSE

In an LSD trance, an ordinary object such as a rose or a candle flame can induce intense visions. In the experiment pictured above, a woman is equipped with a special typewriter designed to enable her to record her own experiences even in her LSD trance for use in research.

LAUGHING IT UP

This cartoon with its wry notations enlivened a thesis by a medical student writing in 1808 on nitrous oxide. The drug, called laughing gas because it often induces hysterical laughter, was considered a mere plaything until its value as a general anesthetic was recognized in 1844.

U.S. soldiers at an Army school in Hawaii act o

VIOLENT CONVERSION

This 17th Century painting shows a grim method used by the Inquisition to wring confessions from accused heretics. An inquisitor *(with pointer)* is grilling the victim. If a victim confessed, he was released, then questioned later to make sure his conversion was genuine and permanent.

COUNTERPROPAGANDA

A U.S. Army poster *(right)* shows a prisoner of war's fist jabbing a confession with a pen as he refuses to sign it. Below the picture is part of the U.S. "Fighting Man's Code." Posters like this one are intended to fortify U.S. servicemen against brainwashing if they are captured.

When questioned, should I become a prisoner of war, I am bound to give only name, rank, service number and date of birth. I will evade answering further questions to the utmost of my ability. I will make no oral or written statements disloyal to my country and its allies or harmful to their cause.

168

realistic brainwashing interrogation scene for an audience of soldiers, to prepare them for what they might meet as prisoners of war.

Torture and Brainwashing

Unbearable stress can be a powerful changer of men's minds. The stern inquisitors of the Spanish Inquisition, for example, were not primarily interested in punishing heretics, but in winning converts. They recognized that the demoralizing and painful experience of torture could produce genuine changes of belief *(opposite, left)*.

Today it is more clearly understood that extreme suggestibility accompanies acute stress of any kind. The Russian Communists of the 1930s developed ways of bending prisoners to their will without resorting to gross physical torture. These methods were widely used by the Red Chinese during the Korean War, when the term "brainwashing" was coined. The victim to be brainwashed is isolated in conditions of constant discomfort. When reduced to a totally anxious state, he is brought forth for relentless and humiliating interrogations. The victim is usually so shaken that he is highly susceptible to new ideas, which his captors plant and nurture with sudden, friendly reassurances.

169

IDEAL ALLIES

In 1950, posters like these on a wall in Pyongyang helped persuade the North Koreans that powerful and glamorous figures believed in the correctness of the fight against South Korea.

A benign-looking Stalin gestures in greeting in the first poster and the faces of two young students in the second are idealized. In the last poster, Uncle Sam is shown as an ugly old man.

Governmental Controls

Probably everyone needs reassurance from others that he is right. When a dictatorship has control of communications, it can prevent circulation of all opinions but its own, and constantly assure the public that only this view is correct. Secret dissident groups may form, but great numbers of people will follow the easier government line. In Red China, Government propaganda has evidently been so effective in forming public opinion that a nation of more than 730 million has transformed its way of life.

ORGANIZED TO LISTEN

This picture, taken by the French photographer Henri Cartier-Bresson, shows Red Chinese militiamen in a square in Peking. When civilians are highly organized, it is much easier to expose them to constant political propaganda. China's militia includes 100 million men and women. Almost all Chinese civilians are members of one Government-sponsored organization or another.

RALLYING TO THE COMMON CAUSE

At a rally in Peking, half a million Chinese turn out to hear their leaders crank up anti-Western sentiment. Anger at a common enemy unites a people, and slogans, flags and patriotic speeches create an atmosphere in which private doubt of the prevailing attitude is almost impossible.

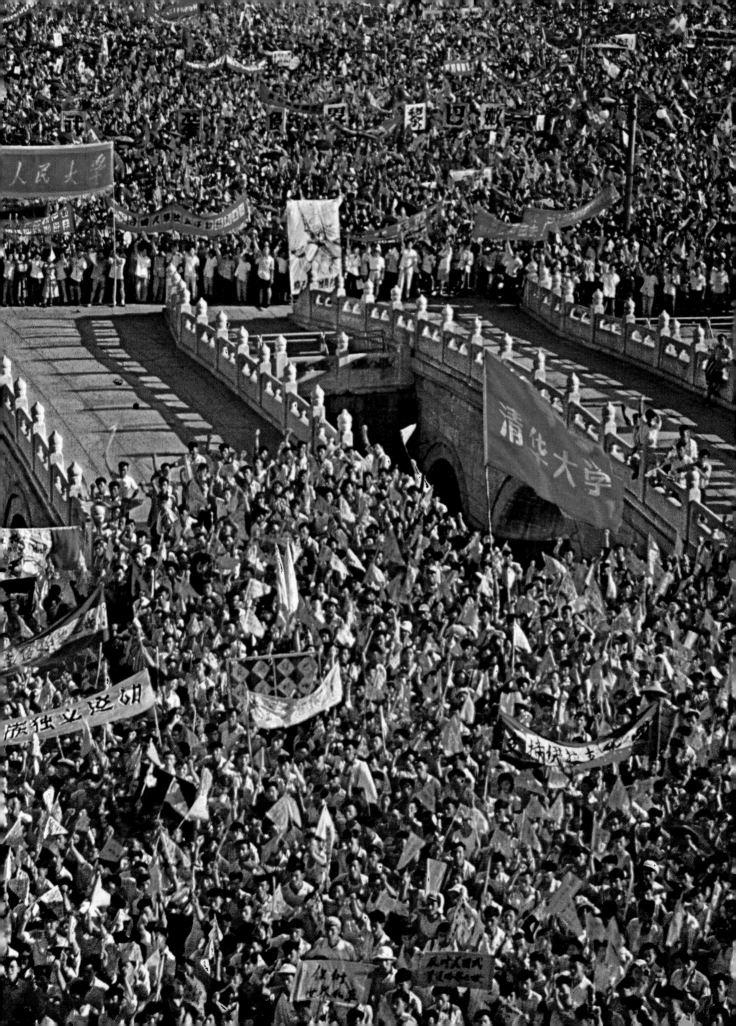

8

Mind and the Future of Man

THE FUTURE OF THE MIND is a subject to be approached expectantly but warily. Psychologists who have thought much about it seem disposed to expect some breathtaking changes in our notions about the brain and the mind, though they are not at all agreed on the nature of the changes. New information may lead to new insights into the nature of consciousness, perhaps the most baffling of all psychological phenomena. It may also reveal a great deal more about the nature of pleasure and pain, about the possibility of raising intelligence to previously undreamed-of levels, about the possibility, straight out of science fiction, of keeping the brain alive after its possessor dies—and still more.

Our new understanding of the brain is coming through two quite different avenues. One is the recent development of extraordinarily sophisticated electronic and chemical techniques that enable us to explore the brain in microscopic detail, to pinpoint the physical sources of specific emotions and thought processes, and to arouse or depress them artificially. The second is the new science of cybernetics, which has simulated the brain in an astonishing variety of functions, creating machines that, in some sense, at least, are able to think and learn and respond "humanly" to a wide variety of situations. The implications of both kinds of research are so dramatic that it is easy to understand why the men working on them are wary, as well as expectant.

The electrochemical nature of activity in the human nervous system, like any electrical activity, can in principle be measured. However, the activity in the brain is so weak that recording it has become a fairly specialized job. Altogether, the brain has about 10 billion interconnected nerve cells, and while not all of them are discharging at any one time, one electrode placed on the scalp will record anywhere from five millionths to 50 millionths of a volt. Perhaps 60,000 scalps together might supply enough voltage to light a flashlight.

The existence of electrical currents in the brain was known as long ago as 1875, when they were discovered by an English physician, Dr. Richard Caton. The existence of brain waves—i.e., *rhythmic* currents with a variety of different cycles—was known as long ago as the 1920s, principally because of the pioneering work of Hans Berger, a German neurologist who recorded the waves on paper. Later it became clear that, in measuring mental activity in a new and objective way, Berger's electroencephalographs (from the Greek *enkephalos,* or brain) might open up a large new area of exploration for students of the mind. But Berger was not taken seriously for many years. He seems to have been a rather unscientific operator, often vague and sloppy in his reports, and quite ignorant of mechanics or electricity, with the result that he misinterpreted some of his own experimental data. Eventually, however, Berger's brainwave recordings were duplicated by English scientists, and the use of electroencephalographs (EEGs) came into common use.

An electrode placed on the scalp does not pick up one simple brain wave, but many waves of differing amplitudes and frequencies. The strongest, of course, will be generated by cells in the immediate vicinity of the electrode, but mixed in with these waves will be others from nearby areas of the brain. Meanwhile, there will be a persistent "background noise," reflecting random and barely discernible discharges that may be still farther away; alternatively, they may be nearby but weak. An EEG recorder may have as many as 32 different channels, but most of those now in use have eight; i.e., eight electrodes are used, and the result of a typical recording session will be eight rather wobbly lines. Each line must be broken down into its component waves, and there may be 30 or more waves represented in each wobbly "compound curve."

A fantastic deluge

Thus the EEG researcher is confronted from the outset with a deluge of information that is fantastically difficult to sort out. The English neurologist Dr. W. Grey Walter, has observed that "the redundancy is . . . enormous. Information at the rate of about 3,600 amplitudes per minute may be coming through each of the eight channels during the average recording period of twenty minutes; so the total information in a routine record may be represented by more than half a million numbers; yet the usual description of a record consists only of a few sentences. Only rarely does an observer use more than one-hundredth of one percent of the available information."

Confronted with "the problem of redundancy" and unable to synthesize all the data that overwhelmed them, EEG researchers for many years had some difficulty finding practical applications of their work. To be sure, they could tell when gross and unambiguous damage had been inflicted on the brain, and they did in fact contribute a great deal to our understanding of epilepsy. Their readings of normal brains, however, were not able to do much more than characterize the subject's degree of alertness.

But now computer analysis has made the "background noise" largely meaningful. The usual procedure is to take a number of different readings of a subject's EEG responses to a given stimulus. In any one reading, the "noise" is apt to drown out meaningful signals. The computer can rapidly analyze the different readings, and get an average response; i.e., the brain wave related to the response can be sorted out from all the others. Waves are now readily found even for such trivial mental operations as responding to a gentle tap on the hand or to a flicker of light.

When the potential of computers was grasped by EEG researchers, a specially designed Average Response Computer (ARC) was built for

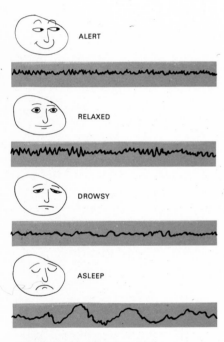

RHYTHMS OF MENTAL LIFE

Scientists have been able to correlate the electrical activity of the brain, as recorded by electroencephalograph (EEG), with various states of alertness in the normal human being. The brain waves illustrated above are from actual EEG records. When a subject is alert, a rapid, spiky pattern appears *(top)*. As a subject becomes drowsy, the EEG transcribes slower and slower electrical rhythms, which become long, rolling waves in sleep.

them at the Lincoln Laboratory of the Massachusetts Institute of Technology. One of ARC's most fascinating and suggestive accomplishments involved the interpretation of data from deep within an animal's brain. A light was flashed at a constant rate into the animal's eyes. The report on the ARC oscilloscope showed that the wave involved in its response could be broken down into three distinct components. One of these three, however, gradually faded out.

The report on the experiment suggested this hypothesis: one of the relatively constant components may pass on to the visual cortex, thereby signifying to the animal that the stimulus is visual and not, say, olfactory or auditory. Perhaps the second component indicates that the stimulus is a recurrent one. The third and waning component may be signaling "unexpectedness" and, by dropping out, may carry the message that the stimulus is simply repeating over and over without change. It may be saying, in effect, that the stimulus is devoid of novelty (or new information) and can be safely ignored.

Closer and closer to cognitive thought

EEG researchers have not yet been able to capture on paper the waves denoting any sort of involved human thought; for example, they have not been able to record the electrical discharges that might be given off by a student solving a problem in arithmetic. But if they believe they are already tracking down such concepts as "unexpectedness," they may be very close to cognitive thought.

Another extraordinary research development has made it clear that the brain's division of labor is rather more complex than anyone had previously realized. This new development, electrical stimulation of the brain (ESB), has proved, for example, that there are many different centers in the brain for both pleasure and pain. In general, the structure of the brain provides for a great deal of functional duplication. In other words, there is no individual nerve cell, or any small cluster of cells, that seems to be absolutely necessary to the performance of any given mental task, and if cells performing a given task are somehow destroyed, other cells are ordinarily able to take over.

The basic procedure in ESB research employs wires that are insulated except for an electrode at their tip. These are inserted into the brain, sometimes deeply. The wires are hooked up to sources of power, so that the electrode can pass a current into the brain at the point of contact. The effect of this stimulation is the same as if all the nerve cells reached had fired electrical discharges at the same time. If the experiment is to be a lengthy one, a terminal socket may be cemented onto the skull; to this are attached wires that stretch considerable distances, giving the subject of the experiment plenty of room to move around in. The procedure sounds frightening. It is in fact quite harmless and painless.

One famous series of ESB experiments on cats and monkeys showed that they could, in effect, be reduced to puppets by stimulating certain areas of the cerebral cortex. In general, the cortex, which forms the prominent convoluted outer layer of the brain, is concerned with the more intellectual of the mental processes. However, one section of the cortex governs motor responses, and by discharging currents at appropriate points within this section, the experimenters could make the animals move different parts of their bodies, or could make them "freeze" in whatever position they were already in—"like electrical toys," as Dr. José M. R. Delgado of Yale, one of the leaders in ESB research, puts it.

"Turning on" emotions

When Dr. Delgado and his associates at Yale pushed deeper into the brain, into the areas governing the emotions, they turned up even more startling data. The emotions are decisively affected by activity in the thalamus, in the very center of the brain; in the hypothalamus, just below it; in the limbic system, a series of structures rooted around them; and in the reticular system, a cluster of nerve cells in the brainstem, extending far toward the spinal cord. In stimulating points within these structures, it was dramatically shown, the researcher can frequently achieve quite opposite effects by moving his electrodes just a little. A current in one area of the limbic system will set off a frightful display of rage, with the stimulated animal turning ferociously on friends. Moving the electrode just a bit brings on demonstrations of affection. In the hypothalamus, Dr. Delgado found that stimulation at one point will "turn on" the animal's appetite. Stimulation at another point nearby will leave the animal totally uninterested in food, so much so that it would literally starve to death if the current were applied steadily. (Similar effects can be produced by stimulating areas of the limbic system.)

Another famous and fascinating series of experiments with ESB was carried on during the 1950s by James Olds at McGill University in Montreal. Working with rats, Olds accidentally discovered that a portion of the brain seemed to be a "pleasure center." It came about because Olds was somewhat off the mark in placing an electrode intended to shock the animal. The rat was placed in a large box in which it was free to roam about, but any time it got into one corner of the box the apparatus gave it a shock. To Olds's surprise, the rat appeared to enjoy the experience. Instead of avoiding that corner it kept returning to it repeatedly.

Researchers have also discovered the existence of what might be called "pain centers" in the brain, places where discharges are associated with agonizing pain, or with fearful or panicky reactions. Sometimes these centers may be as close as 0.02 inch from a pleasure center. The existence

ELECTRIFIED HUMAN
The creature unreeling an electric cable as he explores a distant planet is a man prepared for space travel as some scientists propose. Electrodes and other attachments would control many of the physical functions normally initiated by the brain, such as heartbeat, regulation of body temperature and breathing. Electrodes planted in the pleasure centers of the brain would help him pass the tedium of space travel. Dubbed a "Cyborg" (cybernetic organism), he may well exist in the near future, for U.S. space agencies have authorized preliminary research toward his creation.

of both kinds of centers adjacent to one another has been found in human, as well as animal, brains.

ESB experiments on human subjects have in general been limited to those cases in which a serious ailment exists, but it is now clear that a wide range of healthy human emotions and sensations can be stimulated artificially. Anxiety, restlessness, panic and intense pain can be induced by electrical stimulation of some areas of the brain. More agreeable feelings, ranging from satisfaction to euphoria, can be induced in other nearby areas. Some of the pleasure centers seem to have the additional function of sharply reducing, or even suspending, any existing sensation of pain, at least temporarily; thus ESB promises to be extremely useful in relieving the rigors of extremely painful diseases like cancer.

Perhaps the most breathtaking of all the results achieved by ESB research are those concerned with the artificial stimulation of memory. Here the technique is to send electrical currents into parts of the cortex. This area of investigation is especially associated with Wilder Penfield. The famed neurosurgeon came upon it quite by accident, when he was experimenting with ESB treatment of some epileptic patients. Penfield was told by the patients that under treatment they suddenly recalled, with intense vividness, long-forgotten episodes out of their distant pasts. Moreover, they would continue recalling more and more about the episodes so long as the electrode providing the stimulation remained in the same place. There would seem to be a real possibility that brain researchers will some day be able to stimulate memories of events about which there is some special curiosity.

Dr. Fisher's "mixed-up rat"

For all the remarkable discoveries it has led to, ESB research has some obvious limitations. Electrical stimulation of the brain is maddeningly imprecise; any nerve cells touched by an electrode will discharge, and the scientist trying to limit himself to the study of the appetite, let us say, is in danger of finding that he has triggered pain instead of (or along with) hunger. The search for avenues to get around these problems led to the development of chemical-stimulation techniques. The chemical approach has been particularly fruitful in exploring "neural systems" of the brain. These systems are in effect "circuits" of brain cells linked together for various functions. One of the earliest, and still most memorable neural-system experiments involved what the experimenter called "the case of the mixed-up rat."

The experimenter in question, Alan E. Fisher, is now a psychologist on the staff of the University of Pittsburgh. Fisher conceived the idea of injecting the male sex hormone, testosterone, into the hypothalamus of a male rat. He expected, naturally enough, to find that it would become sexually eager and pursue any available female. But the rat first attempted to pick up a female rat by the tail, and then by the loose skin on her back. He seemed interested only in carrying her across the cage and dropping her. Gradually it became apparent that the male was trying to fill a "maternal" role, even to the extent of building a nest in the cage for some rat pups that were put in with him. Fisher got other rats—including even female rats—to act like sexually aggressive males after they were injected with testosterone at a slightly different point in the hypothalamus.

The explanation finally worked out by Fisher was this: what was crucial was not the exact hormone used, but the exact brain cells it was used on. Some cells, in both male and female rats, are concerned with maternal behavior; others are concerned with male sexual behavior. Ordinarily, of course, the cells concerned with maternal behavior are never stimulated in male rats. These cells remain inactive all during their lives, and have no occasion to develop as part of the neural system that is associated with female behavior generally. Fisher concluded, from this and other studies, that these systems in the brain tend to develop most fully when they are activated by hormones early in life. Indeed, he suggested the general rule that, in every species, the gross patterns of male and female behavior are importantly affected by chemical stimulation of certain nerve sections at early ages. This, of course, suggests that deviant sexual behavior in humans, as well as animals, may proceed from chemical deficiencies during the period of youth.

Interchanges in the brain

In another experiment, Fisher and a colleague, John N. Coury, found that they could get rats to drink tremendous quantities of water by injecting their brains with acetylcholine. These injections could be made at a sizable number of points in the brain's limbic system. In other words, there was a "thirst circuit." Fisher described the effect of injecting three different chemicals into the brain of a male rat at a point in the brain that was plainly an "interchange" for several different circuits. "An injection of acetylcholine into this site stimulated him to drink, noradrenaline prompted him to eat and testosterone caused him to build nests."

Our expanded understanding of the brain comes not only from chemical and electronic research but also from successful efforts to simulate the brain's operations with computers. More and more of the brain's functions have now been duplicated by computers. Like the brain, computers can of course be used to solve mathematical and other logical problems. Both brains and computers are, in effect, able to process the raw material of information they receive and to sort out what is relevant in a particular situation from what is not. Both work on electrical circuits; indeed, the brain's nerve cells are often compared to vacuum tubes, which can be turned on and off to govern the flow of electricity through a circuit. Both brains and computers have fairly elaborate procedures for making sure that errors do not occur in their calculations. The brain does this by recording the evidence of several different human senses on millions of different nerve cells, and noting whether there seem to be inconsistencies, while some computers have built-in "memory" devices to ensure that the data from past operations are consistent with more recent data. And computers are becoming more and more successful at making predictions, something the brain has been doing for a long time.

There is, to be sure, an extraordinary difference in the capacities of the brain and the computers. While all computers can solve some kinds of problems better than the brain, none of them has the brain's fantastic capacity to store information. Dr. Walter, perhaps the leading authority on duplicating brain functions mechanically, has succeeded in constructing electric models of brain cells. He has declared, however, that the cost of wiring them so that they are interconnected as cells are in the brain would be wildly uneconomical.

But Walter and others have pushed ahead with projects to produce a model of the brain that simulates many of its capabilities. Walter began by hypothesizing that cerebral functions might be duplicated with far fewer units than the total number of cells in the brain, provided only that the units used were elaborately and intricately interconnected. The final product of his and others' labors is a device christened *Machina speculatrix*, also known as *M. speculatrix*. One of them, known more intimately as Elsie, is shown and described in the picture essay which follows this chapter. Dr. Walter speaks of this and similar machines as "creatures," and has said that devices of this kind can be constructed that will be capable of a "mimicry of life [that] will be valid and illuminating."

Are they creatures?

It can be argued that, while such machines may indeed "mimic" life, they are not really "creatures" because they lack the essential ingredient of living creatures, i.e., a sense of consciousness. This is a matter about which students of the brain are in disagreement. Some of them feel that consciousness itself presents no particular problem to a "mechanistic" view of the brain. Dean Wooldridge, the distinguished American scientist, and one of the founders of Thompson Ramo Wooldridge, the giant electronics company, has argued in *The Machinery of the Brain* that we may soon come "to accept the sense of consciousness itself as a natural

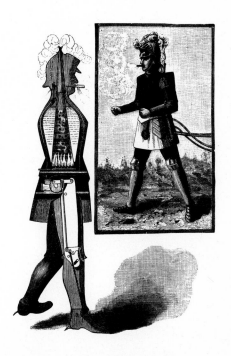

THE WALKING TIN MAN
Before man invented electronic computers that imitate the workings of his mind, he built mechanical devices that imitated his physical actions. This 19th Century picture is of a steam man that was built in Canada. A half-horsepower motor drove jointed rods which moved the robot's legs. Attached to a horizontal bar, it could walk in circles. A small exhaust pipe from the gasoline-fired boiler can be seen protruding from its mouth.

phenomenon suited to being described by and dealt with by the body of laws and methods of the physical sciences." We may find, for example, that consciousness may be a function of a specific voltage in a given nucleus of the brainstem.

It is true, of course, that by its nature consciousness is something the subject has to tell us about; consciousness is not something another person can see. This point presents a considerable difficulty for the researcher trying to gauge it without depending on another's subjective reactions. On the other hand, the point raises a startling question. Is it possible that consciousness might be duplicated in computers of the future, even if the machines could not tell us about it? Wooldridge raises this question even about existing computers: "Is it possible that, somewhere among their wires and transistors, there already stirs the dim glimmering of the same kind of sense of awareness that has become, for man, his most personal and precious possession?"

What Wooldridge asks is an electronic-age echo of a statement by Sir Charles Sherrington, who was a poet as well as a dedicated researcher of the nervous system in the early 1900s. The brain, Sir Charles decided at the age of 83, is "an enchanted loom where millions of flashing shuttles weave a dissolving pattern, always a meaningful pattern though never an abiding one."

Exploring Inside the Brain

A robot named Elsie appears in this essay, capable of almost humanlike determination. Nevertheless, no modern scientist believes that man is about to be replaced by the electronic brain. The living brain is being charted as never before, thanks to modern equipment and techniques. Scientists can place electrical conductors on the outside of the skull and precisely measure the electrical activity within. They can plunge a tiny wire through the skull and probe among the brain's billions of nerve cells (opposite). What have they found? Among other things, that the brain is an organ containing deep-seated centers of ecstasy and rage; an organ that dreams as inexorably as the sun sets. This essay tells of the dynamic forces at work in the brain that are just beginning to be understood. But attempts to measure them have not answered all the questions. No one yet knows how these processes give rise to a thought, an emotion or a dream.

TAKING ACCURATE SOUNDINGS
A metal "halo," clamped to an epileptic patient's head at Massachusetts General Hospital, Boston, holds an electrode implanted in his brain. A simple ground wire is taped to his chin. By detecting changes in electrical impulses in the brain, electrodes locate abnormal cells, such as those that cause epilepsy and Parkinson's disease. They can then be surgically removed or treated with drugs.

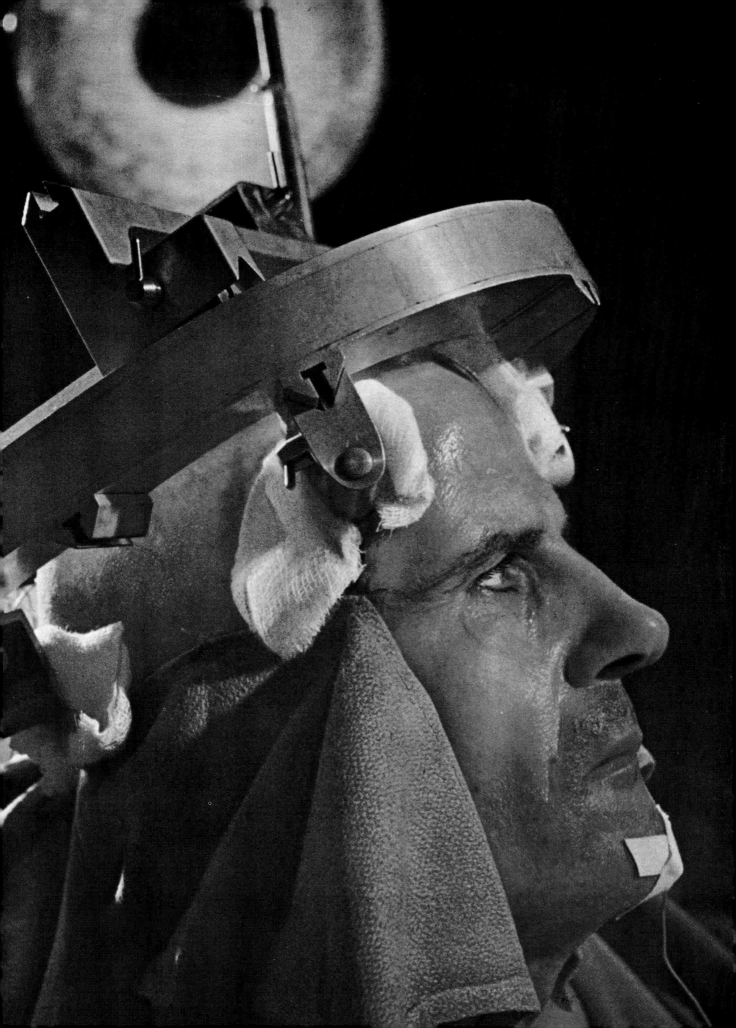

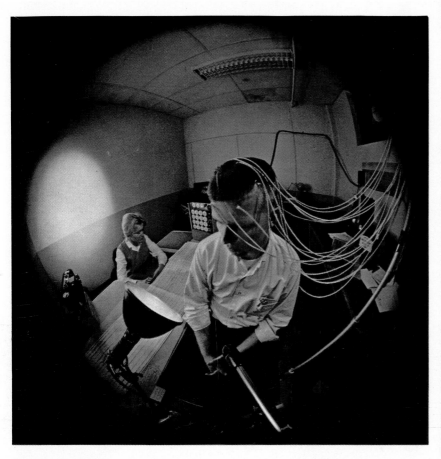

RHYTHMIC FLICKER

Controlled flickers of light affect the electrical rhythms of the brain. If a normal subject stares at a flickering light whose rate is synchronized with his brain's alpha waves—minute electrical discharges in the brain pulsing at from eight to 13 cycles per second—his alpha waves may speed up or slow down. A flicker synchronized with an epileptic's brain waves induces seizures.

TELLTALE SKIN

Patterns of light, like these concentric circles, are registered by the nervous system even when flashed on a screen too fast for full conscious awareness. Dr. James Block *(above)* of the Albert Einstein College of Medicine, New York, has measured subconscious responses to stimuli by recording electrical changes in the skin that occur whenever a stimulus alerts the brain.

Attuned to the Electrical Brain

The living brain's electrical activity was first faintly detected in 1875. It was not until 1924, however, that neurologist Hans Berger, using ordinary radio equipment, succeeded in amplifying the brain's electrical impulses more than a million times, so that their rhythms could be recorded on graph paper and studied. Dr. Berger's invention became the electroencephalograph, known as the EEG. Now developed into a phenomenally sensitive instrument, it measures the currents within the brain by means of conductors, or electrodes, pasted to the outside of the skull. It enables scientists to record the various discharges of energy when the mind is relaxed or actively concentrating.

WRITTEN RECORD OF THE BRAIN
An electroencephalograph records its measurements of the brain's electrical activity onto graph paper in lines like those above. Four basic brain waves have been distinguished by the EEG.

MEASURING THE MIND AT WORK
Electrodes lead from a man's scalp *(left)* to a newly designed electroencephalograph at Columbia-Presbyterian Hospital in New York. This EEG can detect steady impulses of as little magnitude as one 200,000th of a volt, and can record from precisely selected areas of the brain.

183

STIMULATED RAT

Electronic boxes like this one, with a lever connected to graphs and other measuring devices, are being used in many experiments with animals. This rat is pressing the lever to get food.

Rats have also pressed levers that delivered electrical impulses to the "pleasure centers" of their brains—sometimes pressing as often as 5,000 times an hour until they drop in exhaustion.

Probing inside the Brain

Electrodes are simply conductors of electricity. Placed outside the skull, they can deliver currents from the brain to a sensitive EEG for measurement. Inserted in the brain and attached to a power supply, they will deliver electric currents to specific brain cells. The effect is exactly the same as the brain's own electrical activity. Scientists use this artificial stimulation to find out what areas of the brain provoke what responses.

The limbic system, for example, has been mapped in considerable detail by this technique. Located deep in the brain, it is one of the higher centers that control emotions. It provokes an astonishing variety of responses in animals, depending on which minute section is electrically stimulated. Monkeys have been made alternately fierce or gentle, rats have been driven to eat until they are three times their normal weight.

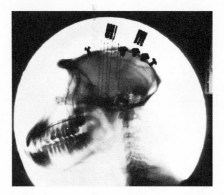

IMPLANTED ELECTRODES
An X-ray of a monkey's skull shows both surface and deeper electrodes. Electrodes one millionth of an inch in diameter have been painlessly inserted inside a single cell in the cortex.

AN INVOLUNTARY WINK
As an electric current flows through the electrode in its brain, a monkey reacts with a wink. By continual probing, scientists have related specific areas of the brain to specific muscular actions, sensations and even emotions. Electrical stimulation in conscious human beings has evoked a vivid sense of reliving a past experience, which stops when the stimulation ceases.

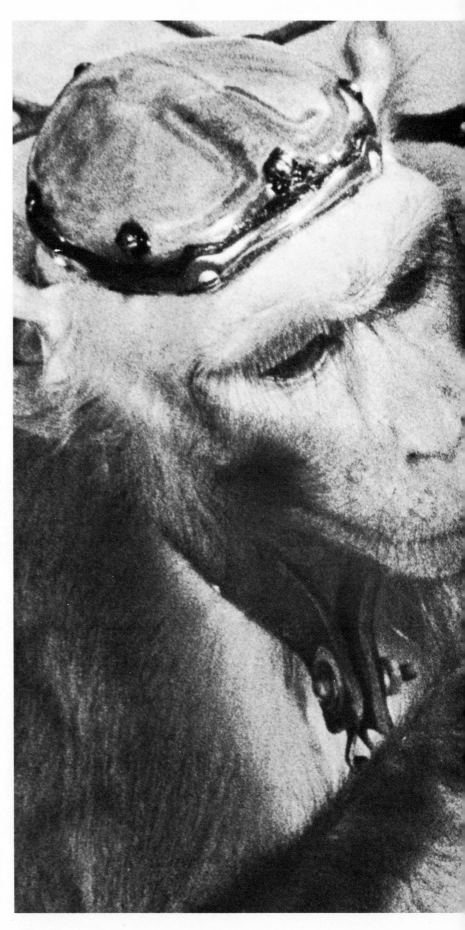

The Chemistry
of the Brain

The nerve impulses whose flow empowers us to feel, think and act are transmitted from nerve cell to nerve cell over a gap of about one millionth of an inch. The impulses cross this gap, called a synapse, by means of chemicals released at the cell endings. The cells themselves consist of chemical compounds. Thus experiments that alter the chemistry of the brain are as important a road to discovery as the use of electrodes.

One subject of investigation is the visible effect on the brain's blood flow when monkeys are injected with drugs (*right*). Another large field of investigation is the many new drugs that alter behavior—perhaps by blocking or supplementing the chemicals normally used by nerve cells. The effects of drugs are as yet more easily observed than they are explained.

SKULLS EXPOSED FOR STUDY
Monkeys fitted with transparent plastic skulls allow scientists to observe effects of drugs and electric shock on the brain's arteries. Under shock, brain circulation remains normal much longer than in the rest of the body, enabling a most vital organ to function in emergencies.

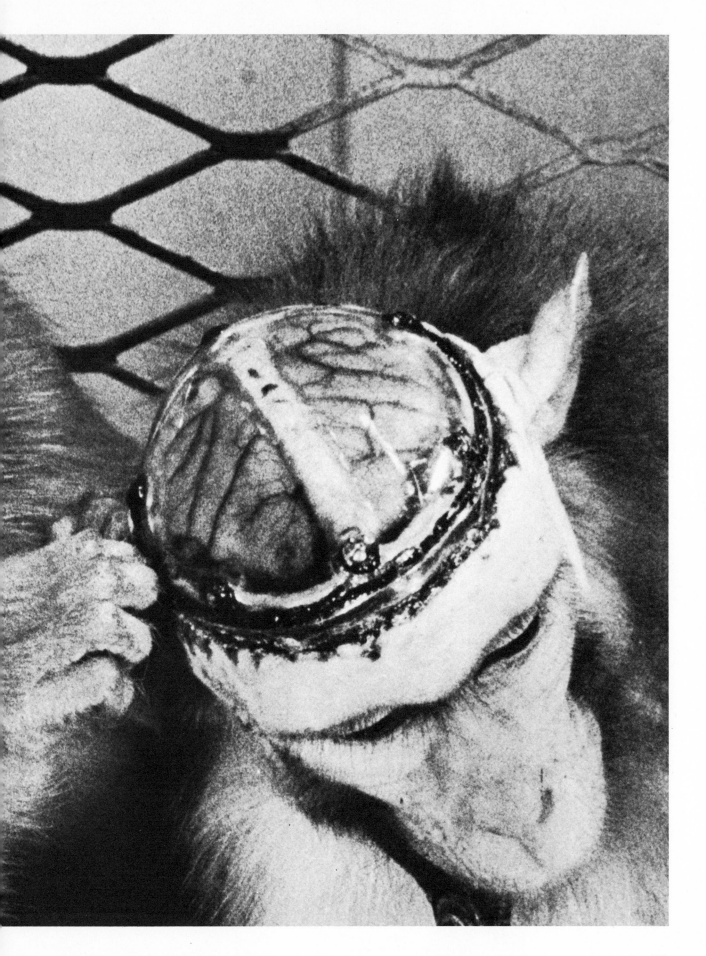

Brainy Machines

A recent approach to understanding the brain is cybernetics—the study of self-regulating mechanisms. While no cyberneticist claims that any man-made machine can equal the total performance of the brain, some find so many similarities in the ways electronic machines and the nervous system function that they hope a study of the former may yield clues to the latter.

For example, both are computers that process incoming raw material with the aid of complex circuitry operating in many combinations. Both have built-in systems for detecting and correcting errors. The many billions of nerve cells of the human brain present the cyberneticist with a vast challenge, but the ticktacktoe machine shown below and the light-hungry robot pictured at right embody in their relays and photoelectric cells humanlike behavior for study.

INVENTOR VERSUS INVENTION

Inventor Dr. Edmund C. Berkeley pits himself against his own machine in a game of ticktacktoe. Here the machine, playing crosses, picks the center square on its first move. Equipped with 60 electronic relays, the machine consults its own built-in strategy before making each move, then records its choice on the illuminated panel. If allowed to move first, it always takes the center square, as would any skilled player.

CHARGING UP FOR THE HUNT
Elsie, a persistent robot invented by the English neurophysiologist Dr. W. Grey Walter, comes in to be recharged after a long run *(above)*. With wheels for legs, a photoelectric cell for eyes and a set of relays and tubes for a brain, Elsie's single-minded pursuit is finding light.

SIDLING UP TO A CANDLE
Guided by her photoelectric eye, Elsie bypasses an obstacle to get close to a candle. A small light, fixed on top of the robot's back and shielded from the photoelectric cell, traces Elsie's trail in this time exposure. Elsie is unpredictable, never exactly duplicates the same run.

SCORING AN ELECTRONIC SUCCESS
By the third move, Dr. Berkeley is in serious trouble. The machine threatens to win on two fronts; only a "careless" relay can save the in-ventor. Blocking one threat, Dr. Berkeley places his last zero on the board, after which the machine examines the situation and then unerringly marks its final winning cross and announces the outcome. A champion in its own restricted field, the machine cannot be beaten, only tied.

The Mind's Active Night Life

Machines can imitate some human functions but, asleep, the mind produces its inimitable world of dreams. One third of our life is passed in sleep, one fifth of our sleep in dreaming. Science knew little of this constant night life of the brain until, in the 1950s, investigators at the University of Chicago found that sleepers periodically make rapid eye movements. When subjects were wakened during such movements, they testified that they had been dreaming. Investigators also found that the heartbeat quickens during dreams and the brain-wave pattern becomes similar to that of someone alert.

Further research has shown that everyone dreams. Episodes of dreaming regularly recur for all, about every 90 minutes throughout the night. The episodes become longer during the night, while the depth of sleep, as measured by the EEG, decreases. In eight hours of sleep, the last and longest interlude may be as long as 45 minutes. As one writer has described man's dreaming sleep, "The nightly pattern . . . is as regular as the motions of the planetary bodies."

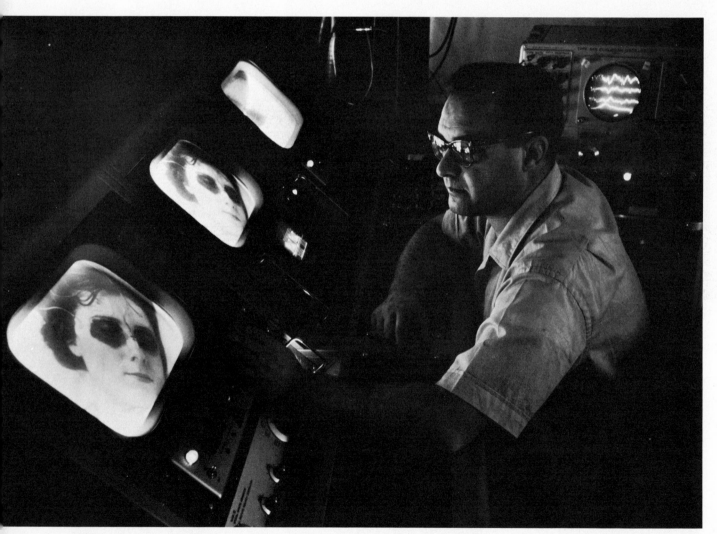

MONITORING A DREAMER

While a subject sleeps in another room, three television screens show the activity of her eyes and body and an oscilloscope *(rear)* records the electrical waves of her brain. These pictures of dream-monitoring were taken at the psychotherapy research center of the Downstate Medical Center, State University of New York, Brooklyn. The project is financed by a federal grant.

WATCHING A DREAM

Sleeping soundly in spite of electrodes, a whirring TV camera and a soft light, the subject follows a dream with her eyes, which have been blackened to reduce any glare. After five minutes of rapid eye movements, she is wakened and asked to give a detailed account of her dream.

190

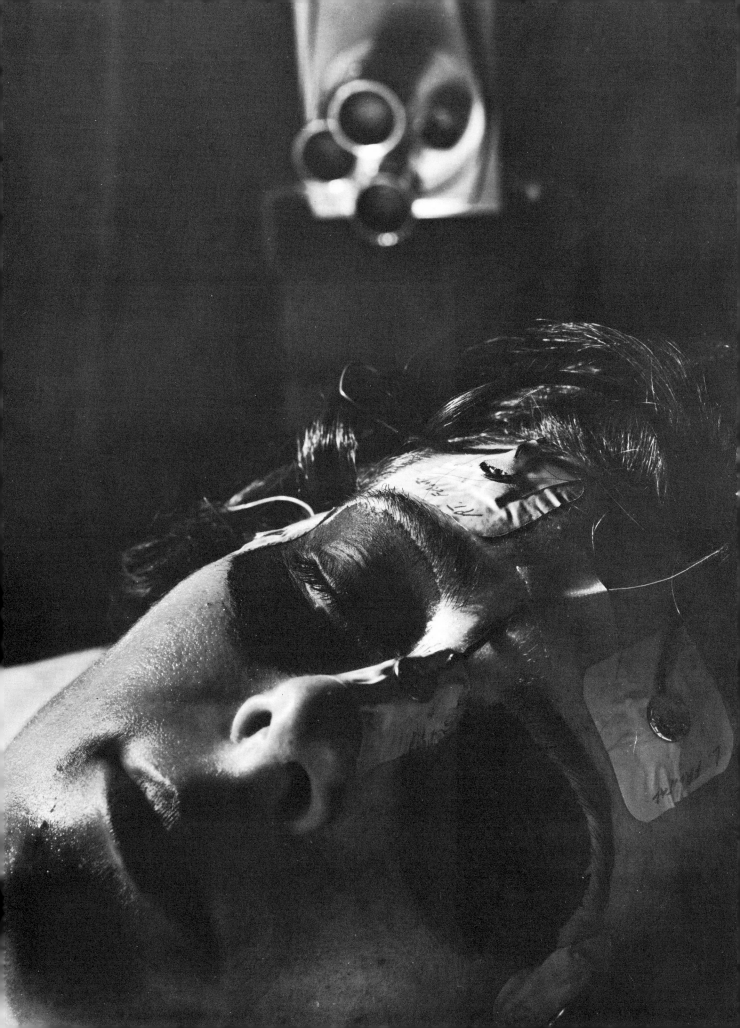

I.Q.-Test Questions and Puzzles

At right are the answers to the sample intelligence-test questions presented on page 125. Questions and answers were taken from a test prepared in England by the psychologist Hans Jurgen Eysenck. It is possible to think of other logical answers to some of the questions, but in most cases the answers given here will be found to involve a more complicated logic, hence finding them requires a greater use of intelligence. It must be reemphasized that performance on this partial test is not a significant measure of intelligence. The answers to the two visual puzzles on page 124 appear below.

ANSWERS TO PUZZLES ON PAGE 124

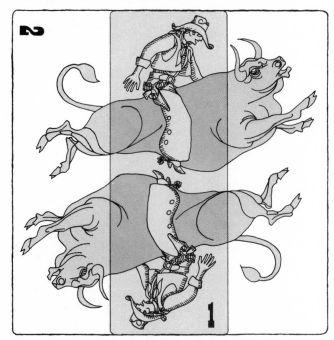

COWBOYS AND BULLS
To seat the cowboys on the bulls, place Panel 1 in the middle of Panel 2 in such a way that two completely new bulls are formed *(above)*, with their legs kicked out instead of being tucked in.

HIDDEN STAR
The mosaic on page 124 has so many lines and shadings that even when the location of the star is known, it is hard to see. It is usually discovered at first only after patient trial and error.

ANSWERS TO QUESTIONS ON PAGE 125

1 **23** (4 is added each time.)

2 **3** (1 and 4 are twins, as are 2 and 5. 3 is the odd one.)

3 **THASER**, an anagram of **HEARTS** (All the others are anagrams of colors: **BLUE, GREEN, PURPLE.**)

4 **PICK**

5 **WARD**

6 ↑↑↑ (Each row or column should have a set of one, two and three arrows, pointing right, left and up.)

7 **24** (Each number is added to the previous one to total the next.)

8 **5** (All the others can be divided into symmetrical halves by a horizontal or vertical line.)

9 **4** (Head and bodies are either white, black or striped. Each occurs once in each column or row.)

10 **R** (First one and then four letters of the alphabet alternately separate the letters in this series.)

11 **36** (Double each number and subtract four to get the next.)

12 **AMP**

13 **O** and **D** (Reading counterclockwise, word "BLOCKADE" should be formed.)

14 **4** (Each number in the middle column is double the sum of those on either side.)

15 **SENSE**

16 **TRADYHIB**, an anagram of **BIRTHDAY** (All the others are anagrams of days of the week: **FRIDAY, SATURDAY, MONDAY.**)

17 **3** (The sum of the leg numbers subtracted from the sum of the arm numbers gives the head number.)

18 **SEAM** (The first and third letters of the word on the left are the first two letters of the bracket word; the first and third letters of the other word form the rest of the bracket word.)

19 **BEWLO**, an anagram of **ELBOW** or **BELOW** (The others are anagrams of lights, **LAMP, CANDLE, TORCH.**)

20 **4** (All the other figures come to points.)

21 **TRUE**

22 **M/I** (Start with **A** at the top of the first "fraction," skip two letters to **D** at the bottom of the next, skip two more to **G** at the top of the next and so on. From **Y** at the bottom of the first fraction, go back three letters to **U** at the top of the next, go back three more to **Q**, and so on.)

23 **NUDE** (The fourth and fifth letters of the word on the left are the first and third letters of the bracket word. The third and fifth letters of the word on the right are the second and fourth letters of the bracket word.)

24 **12** (The top row numbers subtracted from the bottom row numbers and then doubled give the middle row numbers.)

Reflexes, Instincts, Learning, Reason

A wide range of behavior assists various animals in coping with their environment. At the lower end are simple movements (called "taxes") toward or away from a stimulus, and the slightly more complex reflexes. Next come innate behavior patterns, called instincts, then a host of adaptable learned responses. Finally there is the most complex behavior of all—reasoning. The chart at right shows that most species use the whole range of behavior. The graph below stresses the fact that the more intelligent an animal, the less it relies on automatic responses, and the more on learning and reason.

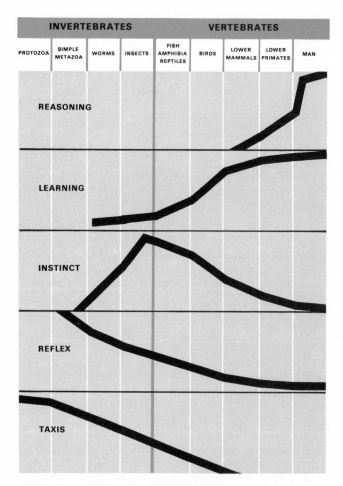

INVERTEBRATES				VERTEBRATES				
PROTOZOA	SIMPLE METAZOA	WORMS	INSECTS	FISH AMPHIBIA REPTILES	BIRDS	LOWER MAMMALS	LOWER PRIMATES	MAN

REASONING

LEARNING

INSTINCT

REFLEX

TAXIS

CHARTING PATHS OF BEHAVIOR
This chart, devised by psychologists V. G. Dethier and Eliot Stellar, suggests graphically the relative importance of different kinds of adaptation in the behavior of different groups of animals. "Taxis," for example, dominates the protozoa, declines and finally disappears entirely in primates.

INVERTEBRATES

REASONING

Reasoning, or the ability to grasp intangible relationships between two or more experiences and draw conclusions, has not been observed in creatures lower than mammals.

LEARNING

In one experiment, an octopus finally learned that while a crab by itself was good eating, a crab accompanied by a white card meant an electric shock, and was to be avoided.

INSTINCT

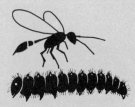

The hunting wasp paralyzes a caterpillar and lays her egg on it to provide warmth and food for the larva. This unalterable behavior is not learned—she is born with it.

REFLEX AND TAXIS

Taxis is a simple movement in response to a specific stimulus. One-celled paramecia demonstrate thermotaxis by moving to the more comfortable end of a tank of cold water.

194

Rats have shown primitive reasoning powers. For example, they have realized that the best way to a piece of cheese on the other side of a barrier was the long way around.

Chimpanzees have clearly demonstrated reasoning powers by using a short stick to pull toward them a longer stick which would reach food put at a distance from a cage.

Man's capacity for using words as symbols enables him to reason about concrete objects without seeing them. Thus he can play a complex game such as chess blindfolded.

Learning without reasoning was shown by a dog, which learned to push the lever of a box to get a bone. When the box was turned, it kept pawing empty air in the same place.

Monkeys are capable of more complicated learning feats, such as moving an odd shape —here the sphere—to get food. It can take up to 1,500 tries for the monkey to catch on.

Touch-typing, once learned, needs no reasoning. The typist is conditioned to strike particular keys automatically whenever she sees certain letters or hears certain sounds.

Birds' nest-building habits are so fixed that some weaverbirds, after five generations of ancestors had been reared by canaries, still constructed typical weaverbirds' nests.

Apes and other primates groom themselves and one another with lip-smacking pleasure. This behavior begins young and is innate, although it can be modified by learning.

Man appears to be born without any instincts, or fixed action patterns. His behavior is determined largely by reasoning, learning or the operation of simple reflexes (below).

A reflex more complex than taxis is responsible for a cat's landing on its feet. A cat's head turns first in a fall, and the rest of the body follows by automatic reflex action.

The act of walking in all animals involves two reflexes: a response to gravity to keep balanced, and muscle movements stimulated partly by pressure on the soles of the feet.

Man has relatively few reflexes, but he does share with mammals the vital sucking reflex that enables infants to nurse. Other human reflexes are flinching and the knee jerk.

BIBLIOGRAPHY

General

Hall, Calvin S., and Gardner Lindzey, *Theories of Personality*. John Wiley & Sons, 1957.

*James, William, *The Principles of Psychology* (2 vols.). Peter Smith, 1959.

*Köhler, Wolfgang, *The Mentality of Apes*. Vintage, 1959.

Krech, David, and Richard S. Crutchfield, *Elements of Psychology*. Alfred A. Knopf, 1962.

Miller, George A., *Psychology: The Science of Mental Life*. Harper & Row, 1962.

†Sargant, William, *Battle for the Mind*. Penguin Books, 1961.

History

Boring, Edwin G., *A History of Experimental Psychology*. Appleton-Century-Crofts, 1957.

Murphy, Gardner, *Historical Introduction to Modern Psychology*. Harcourt, Brace, 1959.

Zilboorg, Gregory, and George W. Henry, *A History of Medical Psychology*. W. W. Norton, 1941.

Biography

Bottome, Phyllis, *Alfred Adler: A Biography*. Vanguard, 1962.

*Jones, Ernest, *The Life and World of Sigmund Freud* (3 vols.). Basic Books, 1957.

Jung, Carl G. (Aniela Jaffé, ed.), *Memories, Dreams, Reflections*. Pantheon Books, 1961.

Physiology of the Brain

†Asimov, Isaac, *The Human Brain: Its Capacities and Functions*. Houghton Mifflin, 1964.

†Pfeiffer, John, *The Human Brain*. Pyramid Books, 1962.

*Walter, W. Grey, *The Living Brain*. W. W. Norton, 1953.

*Wooldridge, Dean E., *The Machinery of the Brain*. McGraw-Hill, 1963.

Normal Psychology

Bruner, Jerome S., *The Process of Education*. Harvard University Press, 1962.

Ebin, David, ed., *The Drug Experience*. Orion Press, 1961.

†Eysenck, H. J., *Know Your Own I. Q.* Penguin Books, 1962.

Hilgard, Ernest R., *Theories of Learning* (2nd edition). Appleton-Century-Crofts, 1956.

Meerloo, Joost A.M., *The Rape of the Mind*. Grossett & Dunlap, 1961.

Menninger, Karl A., *The Human Mind*. Alfred A. Knopf, 1961.

*Pavlov, Ivan P. (G. V. Anvep, ed.), *Conditioned Reflexes*. Peter Smith, 1960.

*Watson, John B., *Behaviorism*. Phoenix Books, 1962.

Abnormal Psychology

Battista, Orlando A., *Mental Drugs: Chemistry's Challenge to Psychotherapy*. Chilton, 1960.

†Brill, A. A. (ed.), *The Basic Writings of Sigmund Freud*. Modern Library, 1938.

†Brown, James A.C., *Freud and the Post-Freudians*. Penguin Books, 1961.

Coleman, James C., *Abnormal Psychology and Modern Life*. Scott, Foresman, 1956.

Deutsch, Albert, *The Mentally Ill in America*. Columbia University Press, 1949.

Doyle, Kathleen, *When Mental Illness Strikes Your Family*. Public Affairs Committee, 1960.

*Fromm, Erich, *The Forgotten Language*. Holt, Rinehart & Winston, 1951.

Naumburg, Margaret, *Schizophrenic Art: Its Meaning in Psychotherapy*. Grune & Stratton, 1950.

Noyes, Arthur P., and Lawrence C. Kolb, *Modern Clinical Psychiatry*. W. B. Saunders, 1963.

†Thompson, Clara, and Patrick Mullahy, *Psychoanalysis: Evolution and Development*. Grove Press, 1957.

*Also available in paperback edition.

†Only available in paperback edition.

ACKNOWLEDGMENTS

The editors of this book are especially indebted to Dr. Jerome S. Bruner, Codirector, Center for Cognitive Studies, and Dr. R. J. Herrnstein, Associate Professor of Psychology, Harvard University; and Dr. Brendan Maher, Professor of Psychology, University of Wisconsin. Dr. Howard Hunt, Professor of Psychology at Columbia University and Chief of Psychiatric Research (Psychology), New York State Psychiatric Institute, and his assistants John Gibbon, Research Associate, and Don Hutchings, Research Scientist of the New York State Psychiatric Institute, were also helpful in the preparation of the book, as well as the following persons: Mrs. Saul Ades, Manhattan State Hospital, Ward's Island, N.Y.; Dr. Richard Alpert, Millbrook, N.Y.; Dr. Richard Bergland, Department of Neurosurgery, New York Hospital-Cornell Medical Center, N.Y.; Dr. James D. Block, Assistant Professor of Psychiatry (Psychology), Albert Einstein College of Medicine, Yeshiva University, New York City; Dr. Harry Bober, Institute of Fine Arts, New York University; Walter Brown, Art Therapist, Rockland State Hospital, Orangeburg, N.Y.; Dr. A. M. Carstairs, Professor of Psychological Medicine, University of Edinburgh; Louis Cheskin, Director, Color Research Institute, Chicago; Lorraine D'Essen, Animal Talent Scouts, Inc., New York City; Dr. Oscar K. Diamond, Director, and Claire Dion, Manhattan State Hospital; Dr. Joseph J. Downing, Mental Health Service Division, Department of Public Health and Welfare, County of San Mateo, San Mateo, Calif.; Mrs. Margaret Farrar, Director, Public Relations, New York State Department of Mental Hygiene, Albany, N.Y.; Martin Gardner; Dr. Lawrence E. Hinkle Jr., Associate Professor of Medicine and Clinical Associate Professor of Medicine in Psychiatry, New York Hospital-Cornell Medical Center; Dr. Paul H. Hoch, Commissioner, New York State Department of Mental Hygiene; Dr. Paul Hoefer, Professor of Neurology, Neurological Institute, Columbia Presbyterian Medical Center, New York City; Dr. William A. Horwitz, New York State Psychiatric Institute; Dr. Nathan Kline, Director of Research, Rockland State Hospital; Dr. Timothy Leary, Millbrook, N.Y.; Dr. Nolan D. C. Lewis, Frederick, Md.; Dr. W. T. Liberson, Chief, Physical Medicine and Rehabilitation Service, Veterans Administration Hospital, Hines, Ill.; Dr. Dusan Mavrovic, Manhattan State Hospital; Rheem Manufacturing Company, New York City; Charles Romaniello, Realist Inc., New Rochelle, N.Y.; Dr. Bernard Seidenberg, Department of Psychology, Brooklyn College, Brooklyn, N.Y.; Dr. Arthur Shapiro, Director of Psychophysiology Laboratory, Downstate Medical Center, State University of New York, Brooklyn, N.Y.; Dr. Herbert Spiegel, Associate in Psychiatry, Columbia University, College of Physicians and Surgeons; Dr. Daniel D. Sparks, Manhattan State Hospital; Leon Summit, Editor, *Spectrum*, Charles Pfizer and Co., Inc., New York City; Dr. Loh Seng Tsai, Professor of Psychology, Tulane University, New Orleans; Dr. C. E. Hedgman Turner, Consultant Psychiatrist, The Towers Hospital, Leicester, England; Dr. Roman Vishniac, Professor of Biology, Albert Einstein College of Medicine, Yeshiva University; and Dr. Henry J. Zeiter, Stockton, Calif.

INDEX

Numerals in italics indicate a photograph or painting of the subject mentioned.

PICTURE CREDITS

The sources for the illustrations which appear in this book are shown below. Credits for pictures from left to right are separated by commas, from top to bottom by dashes.

Cover—Burk Uzzle

CHAPTER 1: 8—Ted Polumbaum. 11—Courtesy The British Museum. 15—Reprinted with permission of Boring, Langfeld and Weld, *Foundations of Psychology* © 1948, New York, John Wiley and Sons. 17—Yale Joel; overlay by Joseph Lambandero. 18, 19—Drawings by Joseph Lambandero—Yale Joel except second from right, Yale Joel from facsimile of manuscript of *Three Bagatelles* by John Cooper © John Cooper, November 1960. 20, 21—Drawings by Joseph Lambandero. 22, 23—Yale Joel; drawings by Joseph Lambandero. Gatefold 24 through 29—Yale Joel; drawings by Joseph Lambandero.

CHAPTER 2: 30—Courtesy The Upjohn Co. 33—The Bettmann Archive. 35—Courtesy The National Library of Medicine. 36—Drawings by Nicholas Fasciano. 38—Drawing by Otto van Eersel based on *The Cerebral Cortex of Man* by Penfield and Rasmussen, published by Macmillan. 41—Fritz Goro. 42, 43—Yale Joel. 44—Ralph Morse—David Seymour from Magnum Photos. 45—Ralph Crane, Werner Wolff from Black Star. 46—Grey Villet—Bernard Hoffman. 47—Ralph Morse. 48—Drawings by Otto van Eersel. 49—Harold Lloyd—Eduardo Defey—Conrad Hodnik. 50—Norman Snyder courtesy Animal Talent Scouts Inc., N.Y. 51—Norman Snyder courtesy Animal Talent Scouts Inc., N.Y. except drawing by Otto van Eersel. 52, 53—Drawings by George V. Kelvin. 54—Henry Groskinsky reprinted by permission of Josef Albers, published by the Yale University Press, 1963, from *Interaction of Color*—drawing by George V. Kelvin. 55—Frank Lerner for TIME courtesy James A. Michener Foundation Collection, Allentown Art Museum.

CHAPTER 3: 56—Jerry Cooke. 58, 59—The Bettmann Archive. 60—Drawing by Fred Hausman. 61, 62—The Bettmann Archive. 63—Drawing by Otto van Eersel. 65—Manso courtesy Prado Museum, Madrid. 66, 67—Derek Bayes courtesy Trustees of the National Gallery, Willy François courtesy St. Dympna Shrine, Gheel, Belgium—The Bettmann Archive. 68, 69—Left courtesy Hans Kopezki and Institut Für Geschichte Der Medizin, Vienna, The Bettmann Archive—Culver Pictures; right Derek Bayes courtesy The Victoria and Albert Museum—Derek Bayes courtesy Sir John Soanes Museum. 70, 71—Ciccione from Rapho-Guillumette courtesy Salpêtrière Hospital, Paris. 72—Alfred Eisenstaedt. 73—Alfred Eisenstaedt—Fritz Goro. 74 through 79—Alfred Eisenstaedt.

CHAPTER 4: 80—Drawing by Steinberg © 1947 *The New Yorker Magazine*, Inc. 84—The Bettmann Archive. 85—Drawings by Otto van Eersel. 86—Woodcut by Fritz Kredel. 87—Boris Artzybasheff from *As I See*, published by Dodd, Mead. 89—Drawing by Otto van Eersel. 91—Freelance Photographers Guild Inc. 92, 93—Courtesy Dr. Ernst L. Freud except top left Bedrich Kocek. 94—Culver Pictures. 95—Courtesy Dr. Ernst L. Freud. 96, 97—Edmund Engelman. 98, 99—Courtesy Dr. Ernst L. Freud except bottom left courtesy Harry Freud. 100—Drawing by William Cotton © 1931, 1939 Condé Nast Publications Inc., courtesy New York Public Library. 101—Wide World Photos—courtesy Dr. Ernst L. Freud. 102—Edmund Engelman—Wide World Photos. 103—Courtesy Dr. Ernst L. Freud.

CHAPTER 5: 104—A. Y. Owen. 107—Drawing by Otto van Eersel from "The Psychological Bulletin," courtesy American Psychological Association. 108, 109, 110—Drawings by Otto van Eersel. 115—Matt Herron. 116—Albert Fenn. 117—Albert Fenn, Thomas D. McAvoy. 118—Robert W. Kelley—Albert Fenn. 119—Robert W. Kelley—Albert Fenn, Michael Rougier. 120—Howard Sochurek. 121—Eric Schaal. 122, 123—Top Robert W. Kelley—bottom Phil Brodatz. 124—Drawings by Leo and Dianne Dillon. 125—Drawing by Otto van Eersel; I.Q. questions courtesy Professor H. J. Eysenck, Institute of Psychiatry, University of London, and *The London Daily Mirror*. 126, 127—Drawings by Jerome Snyder.

CHAPTER 6: 128—Grey Villet. 130—Alinari courtesy The Vatican Library. 137—Frank Lerner, Lerner-Raymond courtesy Prado Museum, Madrid. 138, 139—Derek Bayes courtesy Dr. W. S. Maclay and The Guttmann-Maclay Collection. 140, 141—Henry Groskinsky courtesy Dr. Nolan Lewis—reproduced by courtesy of Netherne Hospital, Coulsdon, Surrey, England, and Pfizer *Spectrum*, New York City, from *Though This Be Madness*, Thames and Hudson, London 1961. 142, 143—Derek Bayes courtesy Professor G. M. Carstairs. 144, 145—Dmitri Kessel courtesy Towers Hospital Leicester, courtesy Ciba Pharmaceutical Co. 146, 147—Henry Groskinsky, courtesy The Solomon R. Guggenheim Museum, courtesy The Municipal Museum, Amsterdam (2), courtesy Trustees of the Courtauld Institute Galleries, Vaering Pettersen courtesy The National Gallery Oslo—Conzett and Huber courtesy The Reinhart Collection, Pierre Belzeaux from Rapho-Guillumette courtesy Musée du Jeu de Paumes. 148, 149—Courtesy The Municipal Museum, Amsterdam. 150—Courtesy The Minneapolis Institute of Arts. 151—Walter Sanders courtesy Munch Museum, Oslo.

CHAPTER 7: 152—Allan B. Richardson courtesy R. Gordon Wasson. 154—National Library of Medicine. 157—Courtesy J. Rubicek, *Experimentalni Psychosy*. 159—Culver Pictures. 161—Gordon Tenney. 162—Ciccione from Rapho-Guillumette, *Aesculape*, courtesy Bibliothèque Nationale. 163—Loomis Dean courtesy Royal Society of Medicine—Ciccione from Rapho-Guillumette courtesy Bibliothèque Nationale. 164, 165—Gordon Tenney. 166, 167—Left Henry Groskinsky courtesy Edgar F. Smith Collection, University of Pennsylvania; right Glen van Bramer except top KRON TV, San Francisco. 168, 169—Staedelsches Kunstinstitut, Frankfurt am Main, Werner Stoy—courtesy Department of Defense. 170—Howard Sochurek—Henri Cartier-Bresson from Magnum. 171—Henri Cartier-Bresson from Magnum.

CHAPTER 8: 172—Ivan Massar from Black Star for FORTUNE. 176—Drawing by Fred Freeman. 179—The Bettmann Archive. 181—Eliot Elisofon. 182, 183—Gordon Tenney except top left J. R. Eyerman. 184—Eliot Elisofon. 185—W. Ross Adey—Eric Schaal. 186, 187—Albert Fenn. 188, 189—Larry Burrows—Gordon Tenney from Black Star. 190, 191—Gordon Tenney. 193—Drawing by Leo and Dianne Dillon—drawing by Patricia Byrne. 194, 195—Drawings by Richard Boland except left, chart by Patricia Byrne based on illustration in V. G. Dethier and Eliot Stellar's *Animal Behavior; Its Evolutionary and Neurological Basis* © 1961 by permission of Prentice Hall Inc., Englewood Cliffs, N.J. Back Cover—Bob Pellegrini.

A STONEHENGE BOOK

PRODUCTION STAFF FOR TIME INCORPORATED

John L. Hallenbeck (Vice President and Director of Production), Robert E. Foy, Caroline Ferri and Robert E. Fraser
Text photocomposed under the direction of Albert J. Dunn and Arthur J. Dunn

XXXX